Darrell Duffie
**Fragmenting Markets**

# Darrell Duffie

# Fragmenting Markets

---

Post-Crisis Bank Regulations and Financial Market Liquidity

**DE GRUYTER**

**Business and Economics Subject Classification 2010**
35-02, 65-02, 65C30, 65C05, 65N35, 65N75, 65N80

The author is on the faculty of the Graduate School of Business, Stanford University. In recent years, his research focuses on financial market design. This monograph considers the impact of post-crisis funding costs and regulatory bank capital requirements on the efficiency of financial markets that are intermediated by bank-affiliated dealers. This is an updated and expanded version of the Baffi Lecture, presented at the Banca d'Italia in Rome on September 15, 2017.

ISBN 978-3-11-067302-9
e-ISBN (PDF) 978-3-11-067305-0
e-ISBN (EPUB) 978-3-11-067312-8

**Library of Congress Control Number: 2022944928**

**Bibliographic information published by the Deutsche Nationalbibliothek**
The Deutsche Nationalbibliothek lists this publication in the Deutsche Nationalbibliografie;
detailed bibliographic data are available on the Internet at http://dnb.dnb.de.

© 2023 Walter de Gruyter GmbH, Berlin/Boston
Cover image: DeanBirinyi / getty images / E+
Typesetting: VTeX UAB, Lithuania
Printing and binding: CPI books GmbH, Leck

www.degruyter.com

for Gertrude
in piam memoriam

# Preface

This book address the implications for financial-market liquidity of changes in regulations governing capital and failure resolution for systemically important banks that came into force after the Global Financial Crisis (GFC). I focus especially on over-the-counter (OTC) markets, which handle most of the world's trade in bonds, repos, swaps, commodities, and foreign exchange. The bulk of trade in these OTC markets is intermediated by roughly 15 large dealers that are regulated as banks or broker-dealer subsidiaries of bank holding companies. Many small dealers are not affiliated with banks and come under different capital and failure resolution regulations. I usually neglect those smaller dealers here, although they are important for other concerns.

This is an updated and expanded version of the Baffi Lecture that I delivered at Banca d'Italia in September 2017. A new chapter is a case study of the dysfunctionality of the market for US Treasury securities that occurred in the Spring of 2020 after the shocking news of a global COVID-19 pandemic.

My main subject is not financial stability. Nevertheless, the form of regulatory capital requirements does play a significant role in the analysis, especially through the impact of the leverage-ratio rule. One of the implications of my analysis is that bank capital levels could actually be pushed higher while still improving the liquidity of markets for safe assets such as repos. This could be achieved by relaxing the leverage-ratio rule and increasing risk-based capital requirements. The current rules do not place us close to the efficient frontier of potential levels of market efficiency and financial stability.

I will show that post-GFC capital regulations and failure resolution rules increased intermediation funding costs that are borne by bank shareholders, and thus the cost to buyside firms for access to space on the balance sheets of large dealer banks. Another policy implication is therefore the encouragement of market infrastructure and trading methods that reduce the amount of space on bank balance sheets that is needed to conduct a given amount of trade. I explain how this can be accomplished with increases in central clearing and all-to-all trade.

I am grateful for helpful conversations with Sam Antill, Oscar Arce, Marina Brogi, John Cochrane, Lou Crandall, Debbie Cunningham, Lamberto Dini, Wenxin Du, Elena Dzigoeva, Eugenio Gaiotti, Gary Gorton, Jason Granet, Ben Hébert, Anil Kashyap, Pete Kyle, Jamie McAndrews, Antoine Martin, Rainer Masera, Benjamin Munyan, Peter Nowicki, Romans Pancs, Fabio Panetta, Franco Passacantando, Alex Roever, Brian Ruane, Brian Sack, Fabrizio Saccomanni, Ignazio Visco, and Chaojun Wang. I also rely in part on what I have learned by collaborating on various projects (some in progress) with Leif Andersen, Sam Antill, Antje Berndt, Daniel Chen, Harry Cooperman, Adam Copeland, Piotr Dworczak, Michael Fleming, Tim Geithner, Frank Keane, Arvind Krishnamurthy, Lorie Logan, Stephan Luck, Pat Parkinson, Yang Song, Jeremy Stein, Zachry Wang, Yilin Yang, Yao Zeng, and Haoxiang Zhu. Of course, I take responsi-

https://doi.org/10.1515/9783110673050-201

bility for any errors in this book. I received helpful research assistance from Renhao Jiang, Sahit Dendekuri, Hala Moussawi, Tyler Ratcliffe, Yang Song, and Yilin Yang.

I am also grateful for support from Banca d'Italia, with special thanks to Massimo Sbracia, who expertly and thoughtfully organized and hosted my visit to Banca d'Italia in September 2017 to present the Baffi Lecture.

Stanford University, August, 2022                                    Darrell Duffie

# Contents

Preface —— VII

| | | |
|---|---|---|
| **1** | **The Cost of Bank Balance Sheet Space** —— **1** | |
| 1.1 | The setting —— **2** | |
| 1.2 | Debt overhang has risen —— **3** | |
| 1.3 | Liquidity provision by dealers —— **7** | |
| 1.4 | Modigliani–Miller, debt overhang, and asset substitution —— **9** | |
| 1.5 | Impact on swap markets —— **9** | |
| 1.6 | Strategic implications for dealers —— **10** | |
| 1.7 | Asset pricing implications —— **11** | |
| 1.8 | The leverage-ratio rule —— **12** | |
| 1.9 | European versus US banks —— **13** | |
| 1.10 | Competition and price transparency —— **13** | |
| 1.11 | The stability-liquidity efficient frontier —— **14** | |

| | | |
|---|---|---|
| **2** | **Leverage Rule Distortions** —— **17** | |
| 2.1 | Leverage rule distortions —— **17** | |
| 2.2 | Repo intermediation under the SLR —— **19** | |
| 2.3 | SLR degrades monetary-policy passthrough —— **26** | |
| 2.4 | Repo crunches in 2019 and 2020: Not caused by balance-sheet constraints —— **28** | |

| | | |
|---|---|---|
| **3** | **Funding Cost Frictions** —— **30** | |
| 3.1 | An illustrative example: T-bill investment —— **30** | |
| 3.2 | Post-crisis increases in dealer funding costs —— **30** | |
| 3.3 | A model of dealer funding costs —— **32** | |
| 3.4 | CIP arbitrage could harm shareholders —— **34** | |
| 3.5 | Regulatory capital and the cross-currency basis —— **36** | |

| | | |
|---|---|---|
| **4** | **Market Design Implications** —— **39** | |
| 4.1 | Opaque bilateral trade is inefficient —— **39** | |
| 4.2 | Multilateral trade platforms —— **40** | |
| 4.3 | Size discovery —— **41** | |
| 4.4 | Multilateral trade facilities —— **43** | |
| 4.5 | Post-trade price transparency —— **44** | |
| 4.6 | Central clearing —— **47** | |
| 4.7 | Compression trading —— **50** | |

| | | |
|---|---|---|
| **5** | **When the Fed Rescued the Treasury Market** —— **52** | |
| 5.1 | Still a safe haven? —— **53** | |

5.2       Treasury markets became dysfunctional —— **56**
5.3       Upgrading the US Treasury market with central clearing —— **64**
5.4       Summary of lessons learned —— **71**

**Bibliography** —— **75**

# 1 The Cost of Bank Balance Sheet Space

Space on the balance sheets of major dealer banks is much more constrained than before the Global Financial Crisis (GFC) of 2007–2009. Increased regulatory capital requirements and higher credit spreads for bank funding have added significant frictions to some important over-the-counter markets, especially those requiring collateral or involving the intermediation of low-risk assets. Pre-GFC, banks did not internalize the systemic risk associated with their excessively risky balance sheets.

The higher post-GFC cost of access to liquidity from large banks does not imply that there was "too much liquidity" before the crisis. Market liquidity is good, not bad. In the post-crisis environment, changes in market structure and regulatory policies can improve liquidity by using bank balance sheets more sparingly. For example, banks should in some cases be disintermediated with greater use of all-to-all markets.

An important theme of this book is that the increased reluctance of big banks to use their balance sheets for intermediation is caused in part by increases in funding costs to bank shareholders. Although higher post-GFC capital requirements tend to reduce bank funding credit spreads, this effect has been offset by a post-GFC increase in expected losses to bank creditors at insolvency. Now that creditors of big banks assume they are less likely to be bailed out with government capital, they are requiring much higher credit spreads (Berndt, Duffie, and Zhu [21]). Bank credits spreads set a lower bound on the extra return (above and beyond the fair market return) that banks must earn on their trading activities to compensate their shareholders for the use of space on their balance sheets (Andersen, Duffie, and Song [10]). This frictional wedge on bank-intermediated trade would apply even if there are no regulatory capital requirements.

This chapter lays out the main ideas of the book, based largely on the concept of debt overhang. Chapter 2 goes into more depth regarding the implications of the leverage ratio rule for the intermediation of safe assets such as Treasury repos. Chapter 3 explains the impact of funding costs on bank shareholders, including an illustrative case study of the implications for arbitrage bounds on the cross-currency basis. Chapter 4 discusses how financial markets can be redesigned to improve market efficiency and reduce the amount of bank balance sheet space required to handle a given amount of trade. Some of the recommended changes in market design would also promote greater competition and netting efficiencies by making greater use of multilateral trade platforms and financial market infrastructure.

As a motivating case study, Chapter 5 diagnoses the episode of Treasury market dysfunctionality that was triggered by the March 12, 2020 declaration of the World Health Organization that COVID-19 had become a global pandemic. This triggered a flood of demands by investors to sell Treasury securities. Because of the cost to the shareholders of large dealer banks of expanding their balance sheets to accommodate these investors, the cost of trading Treasury securities soared. Chapter 5 also discusses approaches to mitigating future such episodes of market dysfunctionality.

https://doi.org/10.1515/9783110673050-001

## 1.1 The setting

Dealers provide liquidity to financial markets by offering to buy what others wish to sell, and to sell what others wish to buy. Dealer intermediation is especially important in over-the-counter (OTC) markets, where ultimate investors may find it costly or slow to arrange trades directly with each other. Most trade in bond, swap, and foreign exchange markets is intermediated by a small number of large dealer banks.

Before the financial crisis, dealer banks kept large market-making inventories and were ready to quickly make additional space on their balance sheets for clients who wished to liquidate their asset positions. Capital requirements, however, were too low. By absorbing so much risk relative to their capital, most major dealers were a menace to financial stability [58]. When some of the largest US dealers failed or had to be bailed out during the GFC, legislators and regulators resolved to restore financial stability with significant increases in capital and liquidity requirements. These new rules reduced the socially inefficient incentives of large dealers to take risk. These poor incentives were caused mainly by being "too big to fail."

The too-big-to-fail incentives operated through two channels. First, there was the moral hazard of the managers and shareholders of large dealer banks, who knew that the insolvency risks they were taking were reduced by the likelihood that the government would step in with new capital when necessary to avert failure. Governments were frightened by the prospect of failure spillover costs to the broader economy. Second, even if there was no moral hazard, big banks were able to issue debt at interest rates that were artificially lowered through the expectations by creditors of government bailouts [21]. The reduced debt funding costs allowed the shareholders of the big banks to earn positive returns on balance-sheet expanding trading strategies that would have generated negative shareholder returns if debt funding costs had reflected the expected default losses and risks that would have applied in the absence of government support.

Figure 1.1 illustrates the central role of dealers in bilateral OTC markets. Here, all of the trading needs of customer "buyside" firms, shown in blue, are handled by dealers, shown in green. As depicted, dealers can also balance their positions by trading with each other. Wang [160] shows that this core-periphery network market structure arises naturally from the benefit to dealers of netting their buy and sell order flows, thus lowering their balance-sheet costs. Although the most efficient netting is obtained with a single monopolistic dealer, the equilibrium number of dealers is counterbalanced by the desire of buyside firms for competition among dealers.

Chapter 4 considers hybrid market structures involving trade platforms on which buyside firms can request quotes from multiple dealers. Request-for-quote platforms improve competition relative to the fully bilateral trade arrangements shown in Figure 1.1. Even on relatively competitive all-to-all exchange-based markets, large dealers are a significant source of immediacy, as first modeled by Grossman and Miller [91].

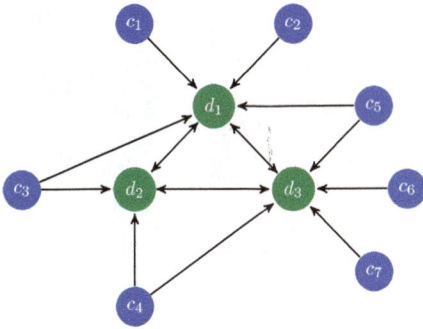

**Figure 1.1:** Schematic of bilateral trade in an OTC market.

He, Kelly, and Manela [99] provide empirical evidence that risk premia across a range of asset markets depend significantly on dealer capital structure. In broad terms, when dealers are better capitalized, asset risk premia are lower. We will explore causes for this dependence. Du, Tepper, and Verdelan [53] provide clear evidence of the role of bank balance-sheet constraints on post-GFC market liquidity by showing how cross-currency bases veer sharply away from their arbitrage-free levels at the ends of quarters, when many large non-US banks are monitored for capital sufficiency. A cross-currency basis, as explained in Chapter 3, is the difference between the wholesale market interest rate in a target currency and the synthetic version of that interest rate that can be obtained by wholesale borrowing in another currency and converting the loan repayment to the target currency with a foreign exchange forward contract.

## 1.2 Debt overhang has risen

Post-GFC financial reform has impinged on the liquidity of some key financial markets through the effect of debt overhang, a concept first explained by Myers [130].

Figure 1.2 illustrates an example of debt overhang in which a bank expands its market-making inventory with funding provided by an issuance of equity. This improves the credit quality of the bank's debt, raising its value. The value of the legacy equity is lowered by this transfer of value to creditors. For the new asset purchase to be profitable for legacy equity owners, the new assets must be purchased at a price sufficiently low relative to the value of the equity given up to new shareholders. For the scenario illustrated in Figure 1.2, the new assets are purchased at their market value and the new equity is raised at its market value. The legacy equity therefore declines in value. If the bank is run on behalf of shareholders, this transaction would be rejected. This disincentive for the bank to add to its market making inventory represents a loss in market efficiency.

Banks rarely rely on equity as a source of financing for incremental asset purchases. Shareholder value is better maintained by relying for funding on the bank's

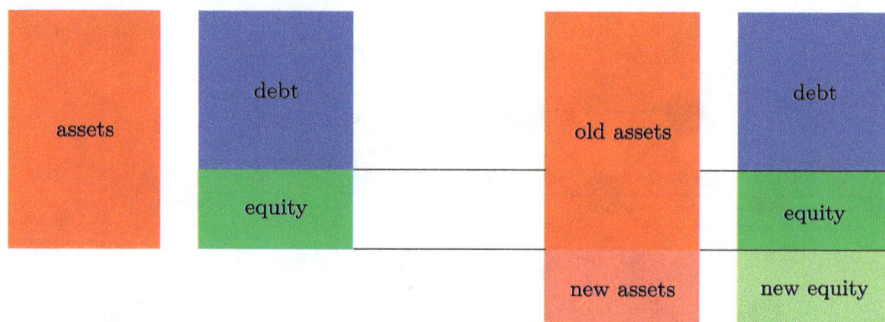

**Figure 1.2:** An example of debt overhang. Purchasing new assets funded by new equity improves the credit quality of the debt, raising its value. The value of the legacy equity position is lowered by this transfer of value to creditors. In the illustration, the new assets are purchased at their market value and the new equity is raised at its market value. In practice, for the asset purchase to be profitable for legacy dealer equity owners, the new assets must be purchased at a price lower than the amount of capital provided by new shareholders. This price wedge is manifested in wider bid-offer spreads, which reduce market liquidity.

excess cash, on repos, or on unsecured debt financing, in that order [10]. Throughout this book, we explore the implications for market liquidity of these alternatives sources of funding, and also the role of regulatory minimum levels of equity financing.

The welfare benefits of a safer financial system associated with higher capital requirements have easily exceeded the associated market illiquidity costs. I will argue, though, that improvements in market liquidity can be obtained, without sacrificing financial stability, by changing the form of capital requirements in a manner that leaves the overall level of capital in the banking system at least as high.

Andersen, Duffie, and Song [10] show that the excess rate of return on a balance-sheet-expanding trade that is required to overcome debt-overhang costs to a bank's shareholders is proportional to the bank's unsecured credit spreads. One might therefore have guessed that the impact of debt overhang on trading markets would be much reduced since the GFC by the significant increases in bank capitalization that have been mandated by regulators. These increases in capital have significantly lowered bank insolvency risk. Once a bank's debt has become safer, there should be less scope for bank creditors to profit from a further improvement in the credit quality of their claims associated with the financing of new asset purchases. Thus, debt overhang would seemingly now be lower. Instead, however, bank debt-overhang frictions are actually more severe now than before the GFC because bank credit spreads are higher, not lower, than their pre-crisis levels.

Figure 1.3 shows the dramatic post-crisis increase in one-year large-bank unsecured credit spreads, as proxied by the difference between one-year interbank offered rates (IBORs) and one-year overnight index swap (OIS) rates, for dollars and euros. A similar profile of increased major-bank credit spreads applies at all maturities. Fig-

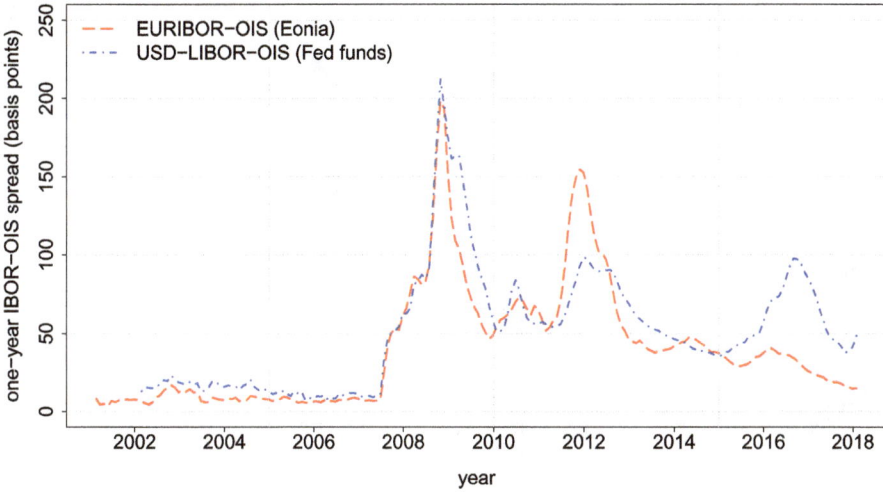

**Figure 1.3:** Spreads between one-year interbank offered rates (IBORs) and one-year overnight index swap (OIS) rates, a proxy for risk free rates. EURIBOR is spread to OIS based on Eonia overnight rates. US dollar LIBOR is spread to OIS based on the Federal Funds rate.

ure 1.5 shows heightened LIBOR-OIS spreads at maturities under one year. Five-year large-bank credit spreads, proxied by the credit default swap rates shown in Figure 1.4, have also risen dramatically since the GFC. Apparently, there has been a decline in the degree to which large banks are viewed as too big to fail. Creditors have clearly absorbed this lesson and now demand higher compensation for absorbing potential future default losses. Atkeson, d'Avernasz, Eisfeldt, and Weill [13] and Berndt, Duffie, and Zhu [21] provide empirical evidence of the post-crisis reduction of too-big-to-fail government subsidies.

New bail-in rules for bank failure resolution target long-term bank debt for losses.[1] As a systemically important financial institution nears insolvency, governments now have the legal ability (under Dodd–Frank Act in the United States, and the European Union's Bank Resolution and Recovery Directive) to convert wholesale bank debt to equity, thus quickly recapitalizing the bank. Governments have stated their firm intentions to use their new bail-in authorities, and have required large banks to have enough debt subject to bail-in rules to achieve a recapitalization of the bank whenever necessary. Although one can question whether the government would actually use its new bail-in authority effectively, what matters for the debt overhang frictions that I have described is whether bank creditors *believe* that they would be bailed in, and thereby suffer significant expected losses. With this belief, the yields on bank debt demanded by creditors in wholesale funding markets are accordingly higher.

---

[1] For the European Union setting, this approach is summarized by the Center for Economic Policy Studies Task Force [34].

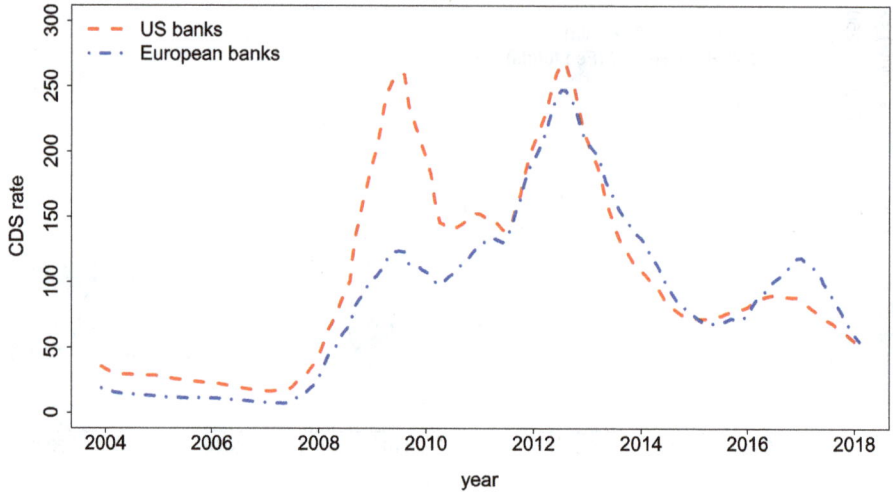

**Figure 1.4:** Five-year CDS rates of major dealers. Averages of the 5-year CDS rates of five large US banks (JPM, Citi, BAML, MS, GS) and of five large European banks (Deutsche Bank, BNP, SocGen, Barclays, RBS). Data source: Bloomberg.

Indeed, wholesale bank credit spreads are well above their pre-crisis levels, despite improved levels of capital. For example, Berndt, Duffie, and Zhu [21] show that, for a given insolvency risk, 5-year credit default swap rates for the largest banks have been about twice as large in the post-GFC period, in comparison with the period 2001–2007. Credit spreads at short maturities are also significantly elevated, as shown in Figure 1.5, despite much higher levels and quality of bank capitalization. An exception applies at the one-month maturity point, where credit spreads are not much larger now than pre-crisis, perhaps because of the liquidity coverage ratio (LCR) rule, or the assumption that very short-term wholesale bank liabilities are likely to be protected from bail-in.

Even if credit spreads had held constant rather than going up, a given amount of market-making inventory now requires a greater amount of equity capital, other things equal. Raising this equity improves the position of legacy debt, thus causing a significant increase in market-making inventories to be more expensive for bank shareholders. An alternative, which banks have tended to follow, is to conserve on equity and maintain smaller market-making inventories.[2] This reduces market liquidity by making it less likely that a given asset will be available in the bank's inventory when requested by a customer, and less likely that a bank is willing to accept an asset onto its balance sheet that a customer wishes to liquidate through a sale to the bank. The shadow price of access to a dealer's balance sheet, in this sense, is described by some practitioners as the "cost of balance sheet space."

---

**2** See Comerton-Forde, Hendershott, Jones, Moulton, and Seasholes [43].

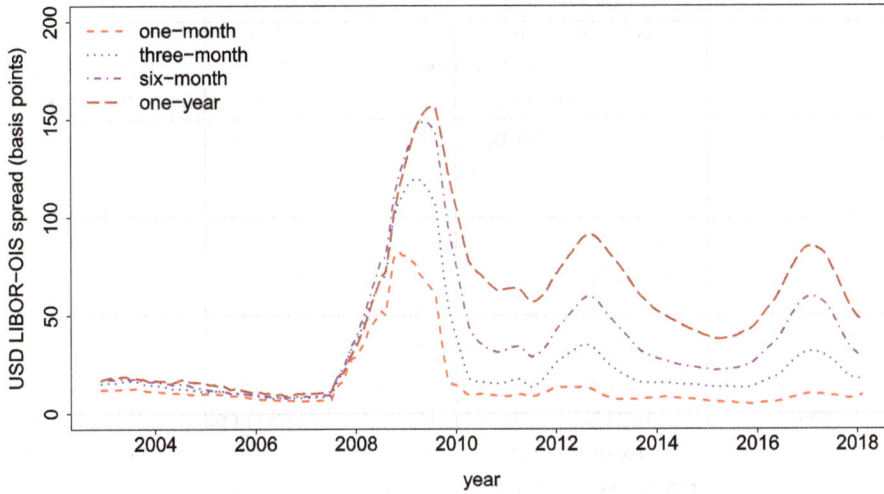

**Figure 1.5:** Spreads of US dollars LIBOR relative to overnight-index swap (OIS) rates (based on the underlying one-day federal funds rate) at maturities of one month, three months, six months, and one year. Data source: Bloomberg.

In summary, although bank capital requirements are much higher than pre-GFC, large-bank funding credit spreads are higher than before the crisis because of a decline in the presumption that the largest banks are too big to fail. So, there is now greater scope for debt overhang when large banks intermediate financial markets. The corresponding reductions in market liquidity could be cured in the long run by imposing extremely high regulatory minimum capital ratios, because this would force credit spreads down, reducing the scope for debt overhang. Although this outcome would be socially beneficial, transition to this improved world would be costly to bank shareholders, given the implied transfers in value to their creditors as banks issue more equity to meet higher capital requirements. The interim impact on market liquidity could therefore be adverse unless mitigated by other changes in market structure or regulation. This discussion sets aside the political realities of how to arrange for the large additional increases in bank capital that would be required to significantly reduce debt overhang.

## 1.3 Liquidity provision by dealers

In the remainder of this chapter,[3] I focus on the implications of more costly access to dealer-bank balance sheets for specific trading practices and markets.

---

**3** Some of the remainder of this chapter is based on my Gallatin Lecture [56], presented at New York University in May 2016.

Since about 2012, dealer banks have been assessing "funding value adjustments" (FVAs) to the market values of their swap books. This has the benefit, from the viewpoint of bank shareholders, of discouraging dealer swap desks from entering positions that require significant financing of margin and up-front payments, which impose debt-overhang costs on bank shareholders [10].

As will be discussed in Chapter 4, dealers have also dramatically increased their use of financial-engineering methods, such as central clearing and swap compression trading, that economize on the amount of balance sheet space needed to intermediate a given amount of trade. To further reduce their balance sheets, dealers have "fired" their least profitable prime-brokerage clients.

Despite increased costs for access to dealer balance sheets, bid-ask spreads have not become wider in many OTC markets under normal market conditions. In the corporate bond market, for example, bid-ask spreads have actually narrowed a bit, even relative to their pre-crisis levels.[4] However, bid-ask spreads widened dramatically during the COVID-19 shock of March 2020, when dealers began to absorb large quantities of corporate bonds from customers seeking to liquidate their positions.[5] Even in unstressed post-GFC corporate bond markets, dealers are not absorbing large block trades as readily and corporate bond turnover has declined.[6] Further, Helwege and Wang [101] show that issuers of "mega-bonds" have responded by reducing the sizes of their largest issues.

When intermediating corporate bond trade requests, dealers are now more likely to offer agency or riskless-principal trades,[7] which delay the execution of a client's request to sell until the dealer can find a matching buyer. Again, this reduces the amount of balance sheet space required to handle a given amount of trade. In effect, dealers are relying more heavily on inventory held on their clients' balance sheets, and less on inventory that they hold themselves. For example, based on data on the US corporate bond market presented by SIFMA [146], in 2007, dealer inventories exceeded 5% of the total outstanding principal. By the end of 2015, this ratio had declined to less than 0.5%.

These effects go beyond the impact of the Volcker Rule,[8] which is less concerned with insolvency risk than with prohibiting speculative trading motives. As I have explained [55], the main impediment to liquidity associated with the Volcker Rule is the difficulty of separating legitimately exempted market making from prohibited specu-

---

**4** This is explained by Mizrach [126] and Adrian, Fleming, Shachar, and Vogt [5].

**5** See Kargar, Lester, Lindsay, Liu, Weill, and Zúñiga [116], Falato, Goldstein, and Hortacsu [69], and Haddad, Moreira, and Muir [94].

**6** See Bessembinder, Jacobsen, Maxwell, and Venkataraman [23], Choi and Huh [38], and Dick-Nielsen and Rossi [50].

**7** See Ederington, Guan, and Yadav [63], Harris [96], Trebbi and Xiao [154], and An and Zheng [8].

**8** The Volcker Rule is stated in the Federal Register [71].

lative trading that isn't intended to make markets. Empirical analysis by Bao, O'Hara, and Zhou [15] suggests that the Volcker Rule has also reduced the liquidity of the US corporate bond market.

## 1.4 Modigliani–Miller, debt overhang, and asset substitution

The suggestion that capital structure matters for financial market liquidity is not a violation of the famous "MM" theorem of Modigliani and Miller [127]. The most relevant part of the MM Theorem states that the total market value of a firm's assets does not depend on the firm's capital structure. Even under its own assumptions, however, MM does not speak to the incentives of a firm to add new positions to its balance debt. Whenever a dealer adds a new market-making position, even at zero trading profit, the market value of the bank's equity can be affected by a change in the riskiness of the bank's balance sheet. This point was emphasized by Miller [125], who famously[9] likened the attitude of bank shareholders toward equity issuance to Mickey Rooney's aversion to "pumping gas into another man's car." This is the idea of debt overhang.

As I will explain in Chapter 3, adding a sufficiently risky position, even before considering any trading profit, can benefit a bank's shareholders at the expense of its creditors, because the limited liability of shareholders allows them to walk away from insolvency at no cost. This leaves creditors with a weaker claim. Jensen and Meckling [113] used the term "asset substitution" to describe this method of exploiting the divergent interests of creditors and shareholders. Even if no single trade has a big impact, the incremental effects can add up over successive trades. Capital requirements reduce or block the asset-substitution incentives of shareholders.

## 1.5 Impact on swap markets

As explained earlier in this chapter, debt overhang implies that a trade with a positive mark-to-market dealer profit can sometimes imply a negative return for the bank's equity. An example of this is a pair of back-to-back swaps that fully hedges each other, but requires the dealer to post an additional amount of margin that must be financed. Financing the additional safe margin assets, which are available in default to the dealer's creditors rather than its shareholders, worsens the value of the bank's equity.

For instance, a buyside investor may wish to enter a swap with a dealer. The dealer will often hedge the new position in the interdealer market. Buyside firms frequently post no collateral with the dealer, but the dealer is now required to post collateral for the interdealer swap, whether to a central counterparty or to another dealer. Financing additional collateral causes a bank's creditors to benefit from improved margin

---

9 I am grateful to Rainer Masera for bringing Miller's remarks to my attention.

backing, at the expense of the bank's legacy shareholders. Even if, as is common in practice, the required up-front payment for the swap and the collateral are funded with unsecured debt, the effective cost to the bank's shareholders is significant and equal to an amount known in industry practice as the funding value adjustment (FVA). Implications are modeled in Chapter 3.

A dealer should enter into a trade with a positive FVA only if it compensates its shareholders with a sufficiently large trading profit, which can be obtained by widening its bid-offer spread. This reduces market liquidity. An analogous "capital value adjustment," sometimes known in the dealer community as a "KVA," may also be required to compensate shareholders for using up some of the bank's headroom (available slack) under its regulatory capital requirements. Market-making capital requirements have increased significantly with the Basel III fundamental review of the trading book.

Although FVA practice was first introduced by swap dealers, the implications of funding-cost frictions for dealer intermediation extend to many other asset classes. For example, Chapter 3 explores the impact of funding costs for the cross-currency basis, a violation of the law of one price in cross-currency borrowing and foreign-exchange (FX) derivatives markets. Roughly speaking, the cross-currency basis must exceed a dealer's funding spreads before the dealer's shareholders would earn a positive return by arbitraging the basis. Not surprisingly, therefore, large violations of covered interest parity are now routine, but were rare during the pre-GFC period when dealer credit spreads were tiny.

Chapter 4 discusses some methods to reduce these adverse impacts on market liquidity, including trade compression, central clearing, and all-to-all trade.

## 1.6 Strategic implications for dealers

Debt overhang is smaller for more highly capitalized banks, therefore giving them an advantage in competing for trades. In order to overcome shareholder losses associated with debt overhang, dealers with higher credit spreads must charge their clients larger effective trading costs. Clients are often willing to accommodate these additional costs because they have motives to trade, such as hedging, that dominate the dealer's debt overhang costs. For example, if Bank $A$ has a credit spread that is half of that of Bank $B$, then the shareholders of Bank $A$ can break even with a widening of bid-ask spreads for debt overhang costs that is only about half the corresponding widening of bid-ask spreads that Bank $B$ must quote to its customers. This would tend to cause buyside firms to prefer to trade with Bank $A$ over Bank $B$, other things equal. Buyside firms are also averse to counterparty risk, so have an additional reason to prefer to trade with better capitalized dealers. On the other hand, frictions associated with customer-to-dealer relationships, specialization of dealers by product category, search costs, and

OTC market opaqueness, may often prevent the best capitalized dealer from "winning" a given trade.

In some markets, the debt-overhang advantage to better capitalized dealers in attracting more trades is further magnified by the increased degree of netting of buy orders against sell orders that would be expected with a larger number of clients, as explained by Wang [160]. Some trades, however, release funding back to the dealer, conveying a significant funding *benefit* to dealer shareholders. In swap markets, this is called a funding benefit adjustment (FBA). The dealer with the *higher* credit spread would in this case be expected to benefit most from the trade, and to bid more aggressively. This may explain aggressive bidding by dealers for cross-currency swaps, as explained by Wood [162]. Another example of a funding benefit is a swap trade that can be netted against a dealer's position in a central counterparty (CCP), thus reducing the amount of initial margin posted by the dealer with the CCP.

Dealers should encourage their trading desks to consider FVAs as a cost to the dealer's shareholders. These costs (or funding benefits) should be reflected in quoting practice, and in the choice of counterparty or central counterparty. To create appropriate incentives, the variable component of traders' compensation could be based on their trading profit-and-loss (P&L), *less* an estimate of the incremental impact of their trading on the firm's FVAs. In the case of swaps, as explained by Andersen, Duffie, and Song [10], dealers have instead simply applied downward adjustments for FVAs to the mark-to-market valuations of their swap books. While this has a similar incentive effect on traders, the valuation practice is not consistent. An FVA does not actually change the market value of the acquired position. Instead, an FVA is a transfer of market value from equity to debt.

In reaction to higher post-GFC funding costs, some major dealers have initiated "XVA optimization" programs.[10] Others have significantly reduced their swap intermediation businesses. One of these, Deutsche Bank, eliminated most of its single-name CDS trading. Debt overhang costs to shareholders are roughly proportional to dealer credit spreads, as shown in Chapter 3. In recent years, Deutsche Bank and Credit Suisse have had relatively high credit spreads in comparison with some other major dealers, and therefore have had a natural focus on restructuring their balance-sheet intensive intermediation businesses given the higher funding costs borne by their shareholders.

## 1.7 Asset pricing implications

Adrian, Etula, and Muir [4] and Brunnermeier and Pedersen [30] examined the impact of dealer capital structure on asset price behavior. Empirical studies by Adrian,

---

**10** See Sherif [144] and Sherif [145].

Moench, and Shin [2] and He, Kelly, and Manela [99] have also shown that the expected returns of traded assets are sensitive to dealer capitalization and to the sizes of dealer market-making inventories.

Debt overhang has specific theoretical and practical implications for asset pricing. Chapter 2 illustrates the implications for the pricing of Treasury repos. In Chapter 3, we discuss the impact of debt-overhang funding costs on interest rate swaps, credit default swaps, and cross-currency bases.[11] Chapter 5 explains how, in March–April 2020, dealer balance-sheet costs generated dramatic adverse impacts on the liquidity, prices, and volatility of Treasury securities.

## 1.8 The leverage-ratio rule

The leverage-ratio rule is a parallel system of Basel-based capital requirements that are not sensitive to the riskiness of a bank's assets. Under the US supplementary leverage-ratio rule (SLR), for example, the largest US dealers are subject to a 5 % leverage ratio. This means that for every $100 million of additional assets, a dealer is required to have an additional $5 million of capital, regardless of the riskiness of the assets. Under this rule, intermediating safe assets such as US Treasury repos requires a lot of capital relative to the tiny risks involved, and thus improves the position of the bank's unsecured legacy creditors.

As explained in Chapter 2, because of the leverage-ratio rule, dealers have increased their bid-ask spreads on repo intermediation enough to overcome the debt-overhang cost to their shareholders. Since the introduction of the SLR, bid-ask spreads for trade between different segments of the US Treasury repo market increased from around 3 basis points to over 16 basis points in late 2016, then dropping somewhat with the reform of money market mutual funds. As a consequence, volumes of trade in Treasury repos have dropped precipitously, especially in the interdealer repo market, as shown by Martin [123].

The SLR has also dampened the incentives for dealer banks to provide robust levels of liquidity to US Treasury markets under stressed-market conditions, as discussed in Chapter 5.

---

**11** Song [147] shows that "no-arbitrage" put-call-parity pricing relationships in options markets frequently break down to an economically important degree in the presence funding costs to derivatives dealers' shareholders for carrying and hedging dealing inventory. In particular, Song [147] shows that put-call parity must be adjusted significantly for longer-dated options in order to obtain reasonable synthetic pricing for equity dividend strips. He shows that a failure to do so may have lead to a potentially important bias in prior research on the term structure of S&P 500 equity risk premia.

## 1.9 European versus US banks

Since the GFC, European dealer banks have given up some of their market-making franchises to American competitors. This is a natural consequence of the relatively stronger capitalization of US banks, which implies that the shareholders of US banks bear lower debt-overhang costs than their European counterparts for allocating balance sheet space to market making. This is related to the ratchet effect associated with debt overhang.[12]

For example, in 2016 Barclays sold its substantial "non-core" swap portfolio to JP Morgan.[13] In Chapter 3, we show that this transaction can be motivated by the fact that the associated funding costs to JP Morgan's shareholders are lower than those to Barclay's shareholders, given that JP Morgan's credit spreads are significantly lower. Another motive for the novation could be JP Morgan's relatively better netting efficiencies, given its higher trade volumes [160].

At extremely high levels of capital, there is almost no debt overhang cost to shareholders for additional market making because creditors are already so safe that there isn't much more market value that shareholders could transfer to creditors by adding even more capital.

## 1.10 Competition and price transparency

The adverse effects on the liquidity of OTC markets caused by debt overhang and the Volcker Rule are partly offset by regulations that have improved OTC market competition. Chief among these are regulations in support of price transparency. Various empirical studies cited in Chapter 4 suggest that the imposition in 2003 of post-trade transaction reporting in US corporate bond markets, through the Trade Reporting and Compliance Engine (TRACE), has generally lowered execution costs for the customers of dealers. Public reports of trade sizes are capped at a level that mitigates the cost to dealers of providing immediacy to their customers. Absent the caps, a dealer absorbing a large position into its inventory would incur greater price impact costs for laying off the position over time. Surprisingly, TRACE price transparency for US Treasury transactions is yet to be provided publicly [92], despite the availability of these data to regulators [27] and the potential opportunity for public post-trade price transparency to improve market efficiency and the resilience of market functionality in US Treasury markets, as discussed in Chapter 5.

Although greater price transparency improves competition and lowers search costs, the narrower bid-offer spreads generally promoted by TRACE could potentially

**12** See Admati, DeMarzo, Hellwig, and Pfleiderer [1].
**13** See Morris [128] and Parsons [133].

have an adverse effect on market liquidity in some segments of the high-yield corporate bond market. Asquith, Covert, and Pathak [12] speculate, based on their empirical results, that the reduction of dealer trading rents caused by TRACE may have reduced the intensity of intermediation services offered by dealers in smaller, riskier bond issues. Nevertheless, the overall improvement in market efficiency likely leaves essentially every non-dealer investor better off with post-trade price transparency than without.

Post-GFC regulations, including Title VII of the Dodd–Frank Act, have also supported competition by forcing the migration of market-making services for some standardized products, such as plain-vanilla interest rate swaps, onto multi-dealer electronic trade platforms, where dealers must post quotes in direct simultaneous competition with each other. Prior to these regulations, multi-dealer OTC-market trade platforms were used primarily for interdealer trade. In the European Union, the Markets in Financial Instruments Directives (MiFID II) require platform-based dealer competition across a wider range of markets.

Chapter 4 emphasizes that improvements in trade competition have not gone far enough. Dealers are still on at least one side of most trades in many OTC markets whose efficiency could benefit from all-to-all trade.[14] Almost all off-the-run US Treasury security transactions have a dealer on at least one side of the trade, leaving significant room for all-to-all trade platforms to improve trade matching efficiency and the resilience of US Treasury markets, as discussed in Chapter 5.

## 1.11 The stability-liquidity efficient frontier

There is a clear opportunity for adjustments to leverage-based capital requirements that would achieve more financial stability for the same level of market efficiency, or, alternatively, more market efficiency for the same level of financial stability. Relaxing the leverage-ratio rule for extremely safe and economically important intermediation activities, such as conservatively managed matched-book dealing in Treasury repos, would have essentially no impact on the stability of large bank-affiliated dealers and would alleviate an important distortion in this critical market.[15] As emphasized in Duffie and Krishnamurthy [60], the leverage rule impinges on the liquidity of the US Treasury repo market, and therefore on the pass-through efficiency of US monetary policy. The leverage ratio rule also degrades the liquidity of Treasuries markets because the Treasury repo market anchors the financing and hedging needs of investors in US Treasury securities.

---

**14** I have a potential conflict of interest on this topic, having served as an expert in private litigation involving allegations that large dealers conspired to suppress all-to-all trade in swap markets.

**15** This is consistent with the "congruence principle" of Metrick and Tarullo [124], who use Treasury repos as a case example.

The Bank of England recognized the unintended adverse consequences for market efficiency caused by applying the leverage-ratio rule to central bank deposits and responded by exempting central bank deposits from this capital requirement. In order to maintain total bank capitalization after this change, the minimum capital required under the leverage rule for the remainder of bank assets was correspondingly raised. The Federal Reserve exempted central bank deposits and Treasury securities from the SLR between April 2020 and April 2021 in order to mitigate the dysfunctionality of US financial markets caused by the COVID-19 shock.

An alternative route toward the efficient regulatory frontier would be via an increase in the risk-weighted-asset (RWA) capital requirements of large banks, enough that the leverage-ratio rule has no significant likelihood of becoming a binding constraint on a dealer bank's capital, even under regulatory stress tests. While imperfect and subject to incentive concerns, RWA capital requirements are less distortionary than the leverage-ratio rule, and are at least as effective in promoting financial stability if set conservatively.

Suppose there remains a concern among regulators that even their best efforts to adjust RWA-based capital requirements fail to properly account for risk and leave the banking system exposed to financial instability because of undercapitalization. Suppose further that regulators prefer to have an average level of capitalization among large banks that is based on a gross leverage ratio that does not attempt to adjust for risk. This outcome can be achieved without the market-making distortions associated with the leverage-ratio rule that I have described, as follows. First, compute the aggregate amount $A$ of assets held by the identified set of banks, without adjusting for their risks. Next, multiply $A$ by a given minimum leverage-based fraction $k$ of required capital, implying that the total amount of capital of these banks under the leverage-ratio rule would be at least $C = kA$. One can now determine the minimum RWA capital ratio $r(C)$ with the property that the total capitalization of these banks is at least $C$. That is, $r(C) = C/A_W$, where $A_W$ is the aggregate of measured risk-weighted assets of these banks.

By imposing on each bank the RWA requirement based on this ratio $r(C)$, and by not imposing the leverage-ratio rule, each individual bank would not internalize the distortions to its market making activities that are caused by the leverage-ratio rule.[16] At the same time, average bank capitalization would meet the desired minimum leverage ratio $k$.

Under this approach, some banks could fail to meet a leverage-ratio rule at the stipulated ratio $k$, implying that other banks must have a corresponding excess level of

---

**16** An extremely large bank might internalize the extent to which an increase in its own total assets, unadjusted for risk, increases the system-wide aggregate assets $A$, and through that, its own share of the system-wide aggregate minimum capital. The resulting market-making distortion, while non-zero, is much more muted than the effect of a bank-by-bank leverage-ratio rule.

capital under the same leverage-ratio rule. That is, this approach to the leverage-ratio rule can be viewed as "macro-prudential," ensuring that the system as a whole meets the leverage criterion, whereas the associated risk-weighted capital requirements are micro-prudential. In practice, one could impose a risk-weighted capital requirement on each bank that is based on the minimum of $r(C)$ and a conventional minimum RWA capital ratio.

# 2 Leverage Rule Distortions

The market distortions caused by debt overhang are exacerbated by the leverage ratio rule, especially in markets for safe assets. When a bank issues equity in order to meet a high regulatory capital requirement for a low-risk position, bank creditors are likely to benefit from a transfer of value from bank equity. As a case study, this chapter focuses on the implications of the leverage ratio rule for the liquidity of the market for government security repurchase agreements, known as repos.

## 2.1 Leverage rule distortions

The leverage ratio rule requires that a large bank's capital must exceed a given fraction of the bank's total quantity of assets, irrespective of their riskiness.

This leverage requirement is simpler than the conventional risk-weighted-asset (RWA) capital requirement, which calls for capital levels that depend on the average risk profile of the bank's asset portfolio. Conventional RWA capital rules had not worked well leading up to the GFC because the risks of some assets were badly understated. In some cases, the bias in risk measures was caused by the moral hazard of asking banks to measure their own risks using "internal" models, or with their own classifications of asset types by risk category. Because of the advantages of leverage to bank shareholders, banks would typically prefer lower capital levels than regulators would judge socially appropriate from the viewpoint of financial stability. Banks thus have a moral hazard to understate risks.

Regulators are normally government agencies and tend to assign relatively undifferentiated and unrealistically low risk weights to sovereign debt, a different form of moral hazard related to political economy.

Putting aside these incentive problems in setting risk weights, the assessment of balance sheet solvency risks is a difficult and complex exercise. The simplicity of the leverage ratio rule is also an advantage in this respect. Risk weights are simply not needed.

The leverage ratio rule therefore leaves less scope for moral hazard or computational complexity, relative to RWA-based capital requirements, when determining regulatory minimum levels of capital for a given asset portfolio. However, treating all assets as though equivalent when setting minimum capital levels leads to obvious market distortions. If banks prefer more risk per unit of capital than regulators would find socially optimal, then a capital rule that makes no distinctions with respect to the riskiness of assets encourages a bank to tilt its asset portfolio away from low-risk assets to high-risk assets. This need not lead to financial instability — the required leverage ratio rule could be made correspondingly more stringent. The concern is in-

https://doi.org/10.1515/9783110673050-002

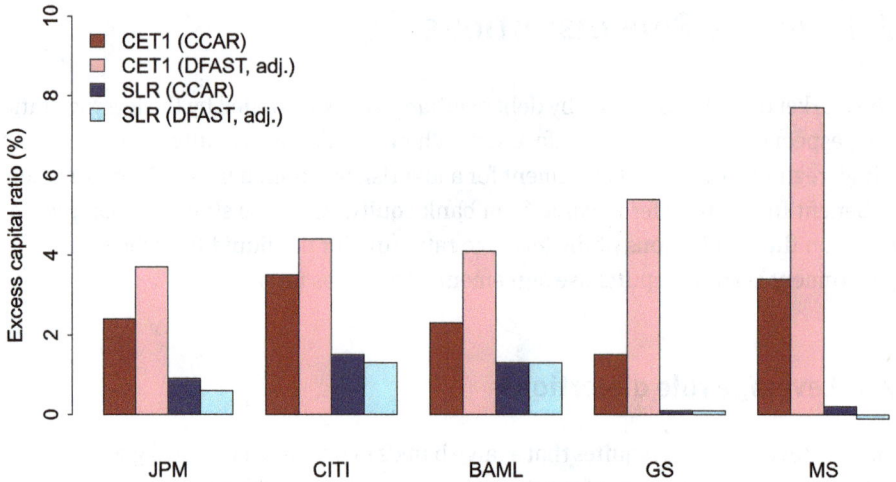

**Figure 2.1:** Results of the Fed's 2017 stress tests for the largest US dealer banks: JP Morgan, Citi, Bank of America Merrill Lynch, Goldman Sachs, and Morgan Stanley. CCAR: stressed CET1 after assumed payouts, less 4.5%; stressed SLR less 3.0%. DFAST, adjusted: stressed CET1 (no payouts) less (4.5% + G-SIB surcharge); stressed SLR less the G-SIB minimum of 5%. Data source: Board of Governors of the Federal Reserve, 2017.

stead that the amount of intermediation provided by banks to low-risk asset markets is inefficiently low.[1]

When the leverage ratio rule was introduced, it was suggested by some regulators that the rule was intended as a backstop, rather than as the primary restriction on bank capital.[2] In practice, however, the leverage ratio rule is sometimes more binding than risk-based capital rules, at least when applied to some of the largest US dealer banks. For example, Figure 2.1 shows the results of the Federal Reserve's 2017 stress tests for the five most active US dealer banks. These stress tests are in two forms, the Dodd–Frank Act Stress Test (DFAST) and the Comprehensive Capital Analysis and Review (CCAR).[3]

For the 2017 DFAST, Figure 2.1 shows the excess capital available for each of these five banks in the stressed scenario, assuming that the bank does not pay distributions to shareholders. When plotting the excess capital ratio (actual minus DFAST requirement) remaining under the stress scenario, I did not assume the minimum post-stress capital ratios actually required by the DFAST. Instead, I used the minimum capital ra-

---

**1** Kiema and Jokivuolle [118] also show that the leverage ratio rule can reduce financial stability by causing more banks to be jointly vulnerable to similar high-risk assets, unless the minimum leverage ratio pushes capital levels much higher.

**2** See, for example, Basel Committee on Banking Supervision [18], page 1.

**3** See Board of Governors of the Federal Reserve System [24].

tios required under Basel III, as applied by the Fed for globally systemically important banks (G-SIBs).[4]

For the CCAR, Figure 2.1 shows the excess capital available in the stressed scenario, using the standard CCAR assumption that the bank continues to pay distributions to shareholders. On the other hand, CCAR-required minimum capital ratios do not include G-SIB surcharges.

For both DFAST and CCAR, the minimum capital requirements are of two types, the risk-based measure known as core tier-one equity (CET1) and the measure based on the supplementary leverage ratio (SLR). For the adjusted DFAST calculation, I used the 5 % SLR that applies to the dealer divisions of these bank holding companies, rather than the 6 % SLR requirement that applies to their commercial banking divisions.

As shown in the figure, the SLR requirement was clearly more binding than the CET1 requirement for all five of the largest US dealer banks, whether under CCAR or under the adjusted DFAST.

Because these stress tests are more binding on the largest banks than are the corresponding ongoing ("unstressed") Basel III capital requirements, one can infer from Figure 2.1 that the largest US dealer banks must carefully consider the impact of the leverage ratio rule (SLR) on their minimum capital levels when deciding how much of their balance sheet to allocate to safe asset intermediation. Figure 2.1 also shows that the largest US banks need not be in similar positions with respect to their headroom and shadow prices for the SLR constraint.

## 2.2 Repo intermediation under the SLR

As an illustrative case study, I now focus on the debt-overhang impact of the leverage rule on the incentives of a bank to conduct repo intermediation, as depicted in Figure 2.2. Here, I draw in part from Duffie and Krishnamurthy [60].

Consider a dealer bank bound by the leverage-ratio rule. The bank must have at least $C$ in additional capital for each additional unit of measured assets, regardless of the asset risk. On a candidate repo trade, the bank would initially receive from its counterparty Treasury securities with a market value of $1+H$, in exchange for 1 in cash, where $H$ is a haircut designed to protect the bank from counterparty failure. (A typical haircut for US Treasuries is about 2 %.)

At the maturity of the repo in one day, the bank will return the treasuries to the counterparty in exchange for $1 + R$, where $R$ is the repo rate, measured for simplicity on a per-day (rather than annualized basis). The repo rate $R$ exceeds the bank's cost of funding by some spread $G$. We will assume that the bank is intermediating

---

4 The G-SIB CET1 buffer requirements vary by bank, according to total assets.

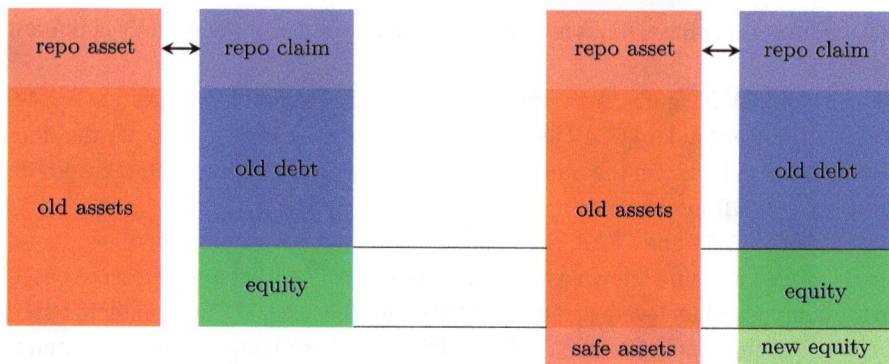

**Figure 2.2:** The impact on shareholder value associated with adding equity capital and adding a low-risk repo to the balance sheet of the bank. The repo has essentially no impact on the safety of the legacy debt, because the repo claims are collateralized and in any case are exempt from bankruptcy law. Adding equity, as would be required for repos under the leverage ratio rule, therefore makes the legacy debt unambiguously safer. Legacy shareholders are thus transferring value to creditors, a form of debt overhang. Shareholders would therefore prefer not to conduct the repo unless the intermediation bid-ask spread on repo is large enough to overcome their debt-overhand costs.

Treasury repos, a "matched-book" activity, so that the bank can obtain funding in the repo market by using the same Treasuries as collateral. In practice, there can be small but non-zero net funding requirements associated with differences in timing between repos and reverse repos.

Repos are exempt from stays at counterparty failure, so the bank could suffer an unexpected default loss on this trade only if, within a day, both of two unusual events happen: (a) the counterparty defaults and (b) the value of the Treasuries drops by more than the haircut $H$. In practice, this combined outcome is so unlikely that an event of this type has not been reported since the 1982 failure of Drysdale Government Securities, when counterparties had simply mistaken[5] their haircut assignments.

So, in the absence of capital requirements, because this intermediation trade involves almost no counterparty risk or funding requirements, it has essentially no impact on the market values of the bank's debt and equity, other than the intermediation gain of $G$, which we can assume for simplicity is paid to equity as a distribution. Because the leverage rule is binding, however, the bank must have approximately $C$ in additional equity in order to conduct this trade. A simple way for the bank to arrange this additional equity is to retire approximately $C$ worth of unsecured debt, funded by an equity issuance of the same amount. In practice, the bank would not conduct an equity issuance for each repo trade. Instead, it would have a policy for how much repo

---

**5** For details, see Garbade [81].

it wishes to conduct on a normal on-going basis, and adjust its capital structure so as to meet its capital requirements, with some buffer designed to conservatively avoid compliance problems. Either way, whether setting aside $C$ in excess capital in advance of the trade, or raising $C$ at the time of the trade, there is a debt-overhang impact on shareholders that we will show is roughly proportional to the bank's unsecured credit spread. Chapter 3 shows that this also applies (approximately) to funding with unsecured debt, although with a different constant of proportionality. With a blended source of funding, some secured financing such as repos, some unsecured debt funding, and some equity financing, because the debt-overhang cost to bank shareholders for each source of funding is roughly proportional to the bank's unsecured credit spread, the overall cost of funding is also roughly proportional to the bank's unsecured credit spread, although the blended cost to shareholders may depend on credit spreads at different maturities.

In our simple example, the bank's legacy unsecured creditors benefit to the extent that the unsecured debt that is retired to conduct this trade no longer claims a share of the recovery value of the bank's assets in the event that the bank defaults. This default-contingent recovery claim is transferred to these unsecured creditors. The market value of this additional default-contingent debt recovery claim, per unit of retired debt, is the difference $D$ between the market value of a default-free debt claim and the market value of an unsecured debt claim on the bank. This difference $D$ is therefore equal to the credit spread $S$ of the bank's unsecured debt. Because $C$ units of debt were retired, the net gain in market value of the legacy debt is therefore $CS$. Given that the balance sheet of the bank is otherwise unchanged, the shareholders' net gain is the funding spread $G$ on the repo trade, less the wealth transfer of $CS$ to legacy unsecured creditors. This calculation ignores for simplicity a small adjustment for the fact that equity shareholders give up this value only if the bank survives to the maturity of the repo on the next day. This survival likelihood, which is extremely high for large US banks, is an additional multiplicative factor considered in a more detailed model explained in Chapter 3.

For illustration, consider an SLR of 5 % (the current minimum regulatory leverage ratio for the largest US dealer banks) and an annualized unsecured bank credit spread of $S$ = 100 basis points. (In the absence of a model of the bank's funding strategy with respect to maturity, I take this spread $S$ to be an average across the entire stack of unsecured debt issued by the bank, assuming that the increase in equity mandated by the SLR leads, in steady-state, to a proportionate decrease in unsecured funding debt at all maturities.) The bank must therefore raise the interest rate at which it offers repo financing by $CS$ = 5 basis points in order to compensate shareholders for the effect of leverage ratio.

Figure 2.3 illustrates an index, called AXI, of the average of recent-transaction (lagged up to one month) unsecured wholesale credit spreads of publicly traded US

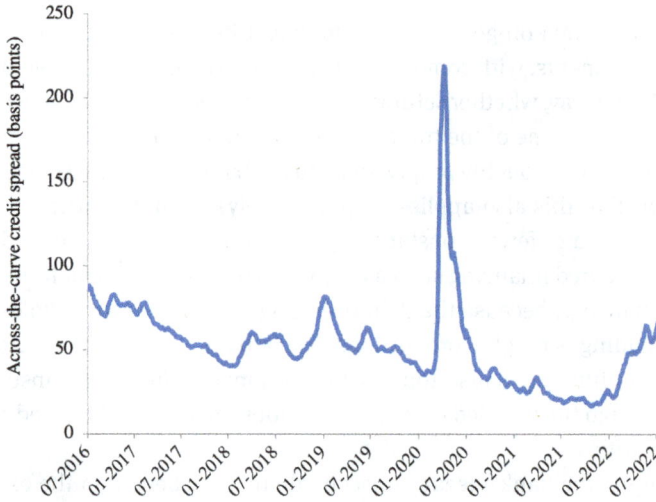

**Figure 2.3:** AXI, an index developed by Berndt, Duffie, and Zhu [20] of average recent-transaction across-the-curve unsecured wholesale credit spreads of US banks and bank holding companies, covering maturities of up to five years. Data source: Invesco Indexing LLC.

banks and bank holding companies [20].[6] As shown, this average cost of funding jumped considerably immediately after the COVID-19 shock. Thus, we would expect that during March and April of 2020, while this bank-credit-spread index was highly elevated, banks had a significantly reduced incentive to provide space on their balance sheets for customer sales of assets. This was clearly the case in practice, as discussed in Chapters 1 and 5.

This impact of the SLR on repo intermediation costs is much bigger than the entire intermediation cost that applied to dealer-bank intermediation of Treasury repos before the introduction of the SLR, as depicted in Figure 2.4. The intermediation cost is estimated here as the difference between the financing rates paid by dealers in the GCF repo market, relative to the financing rates paid by bank-affiliated dealers in the triparty repo market. Notably, a repo asset counts against the leverage ratio rule, whereas a repo liability does not. Since the introduction of SLR, Figure 2.4 reflects a dramatic increase in the cost of repo intermediation by the largest dealer banks.

Beginning in approximately 2019, large US dealer banks were able to net more of their long and short positions (repos and reverse repos) by centrally clearing more of their repos and reverse repos at the FICC, effectively lowering the debt-overhang cost of intermediating the repo market. Interdealer Treasury repos had long been centrally

---

**6** This index weights recent-transaction credit spreads on debt issuances with maturities up to 5 years, with weights across maturities based on total amounts issued within each maturity bucket over the prior year.

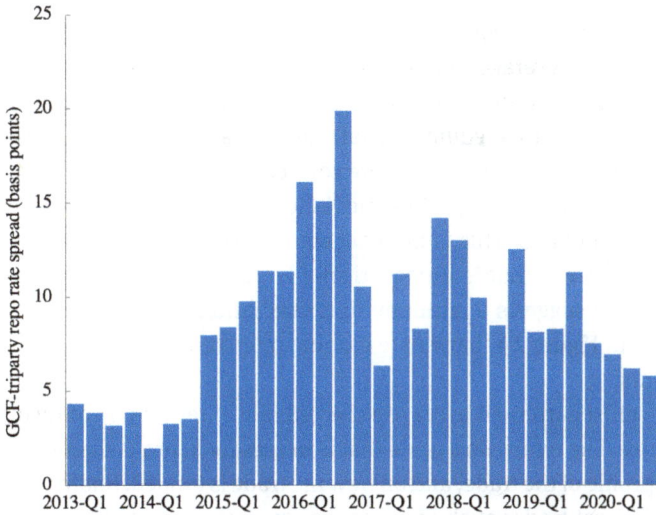

**Figure 2.4:** Average within-quarter difference between overnight Treasury GCF and Triparty general collateral repo rates. The higher differences beginning in 2015 reflect the imposition of the supplementary leverage ratio (SLR) rule. Data sources: Bloomberg and Federal Reserve Bank of New York, for triparty general-collateral repo rates; BNY-Mellon and FICC for GCF Treasury repo rates.

cleared, but customer-to-dealer repos were not centrally until the dealers and FICC worked out an arrangement for "sponsored clearing," by which a dealer could convert a repo position with a customer into a cleared position with the FICC [6]. These novations of customer-to-dealer repos and reverse repos to the FICC offset each other, for purposes of regulatory capital requirements, especially the SLR.

The decline in repo intermediation costs in late 2016 depicted in Figure 2.4 reflects the impact of the reform of US money market funds on the amount of repo intermediation done by the large dealer banks. By October 2016, roughly $1 trillion invested in prime money funds was moved into government money market funds. This caused money market funds to enter US Treasury repos with a much larger set of dealers, including dealers not affiliated with banks that had previously obtained their repo funding from large dealer banks.[7]

The ICMA European Repo Council [106] states that the leverage ratio rule is a major friction in the provision of repo intermediation by European banks. In terms of the impact of the leverage ratio rule on repo market liquidity, however, Europe has the advantages over the United States of (a) a lower leverage-rule capital requirement, (b) a more active direct-repo electronic platform trading market, and (c) a much larger extent of central clearing of repos.

---

7 I am grateful to Lou Crandall for explaining this point to me.

ICMA European Repo Council [106] also repeats a common suggestion of bank analysts that the impact of the leverage ratio rule on break-even intermediation bid-ask spreads is the product of the minimum capital $C$ per unit of assets and the rate of return $R_E$ that banks "require" on their equity capital. For this calculation, a common estimate of $R_E$ is 10%. This rule of thumb, if it were correct, would imply that banks must earn an excess return of $CR_E$ on repo intermediation trades in order for these trades to benefit their shareholders. This is not conceptually correct, and moreover implies an intermediation spread that is unrealistically large. For US dealer banks, $C = 5\%$, so this ad-hoc rule suggests a minimum intermediation return of 50 basis points. Clearly, as shown in Figure 2.4, banks are earning intermediation spreads far lower than 50 basis points.

The idea that banks must earn their average expected rate of return on equity on every use of capital is false. The return on a trade that is necessary to profit shareholders depends on the risk profile of the trade, and on how the trade is funded. Shareholders can benefit from safe asset trades such as repos that earn a much smaller return than $R_E$. Earlier, I explained that the cost to shareholders caused by capital requirements is of the order of $CS$, for a credit spread $S$ that is typically much smaller than the expected return $R_E$ on equity. Conversely, the market value of a bank's equity could be reduced by certain kinds of risky trades that earn a much higher expected rate of return than $R_E$. Nevertheless, this "$C \times R_E$" rule of thumb seems to have crept into common discussion as though it has self-evident merit, despite the absence of a coherent argument for the rule.

A survey of the EU repo market by the International Capital Market Association [111] shows little change in volume over the five-year period ending December 2016, during which the leverage rule began to influence dealer-bank intermediation of repos. Bucalossi and Scalia [31] estimate little adverse impact of the leverage-ratio rule on European repo market activity.

Direct repo, a form of all-to-all trade, accounts for over half of all European repo trade. European and US markets could evolve toward more direct repo intermediation, thus improving liquidity in this market. The segmentation of US repo markets effectively requires the majority of repos to be intermediated by the largest bank dealers, preventing other, less constrained, market participants from arbitraging across the various market segments, and allowing the cross-segment spreads shown in Figure 2.4 to become elevated, as shown by Anbil, Anderson, and Senyuz [9].

Liquidity in the European repo market is also advantaged relative to the US market by the significant use of repo central counterparties, allowing European banks to net more of their long and short positions so as to reduce their measured repo assets. This reduces the regulatory capital requirement for conducting repo intermediation and therefore narrows bid-offer spreads. Chapter 4 provides a more detailed discussion of this benefit of central clearing.

Based on data presented by Martin [123] and shown in Figure 2.5, GCF repo volumes declined by about 30% between 2012 and 2016, the period over which the SLR

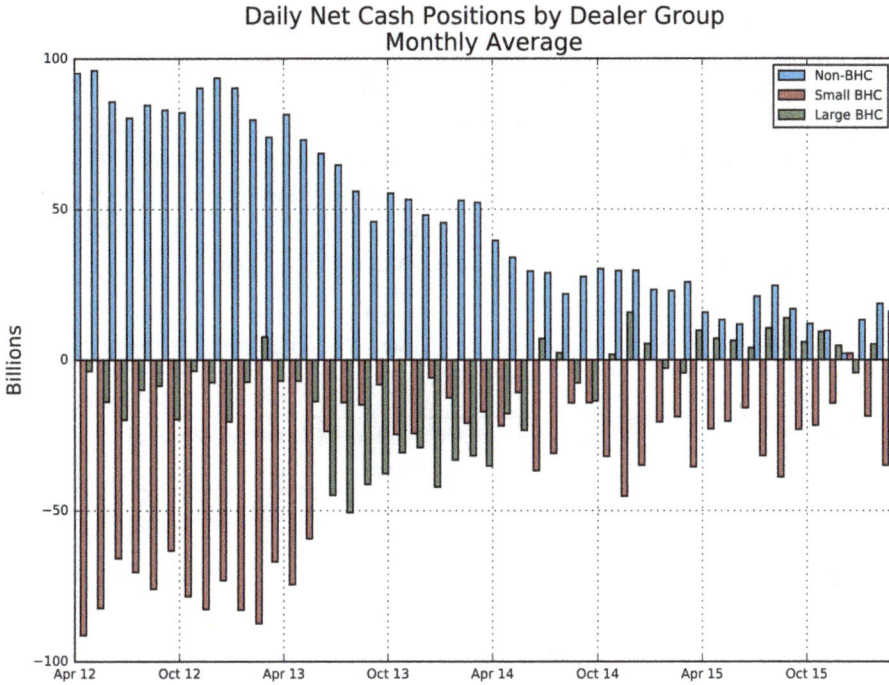

**Figure 2.5:** Daily net cash positions by dealer group, monthly average in billions of dollars. "Non-BHC" refers to dealers other than those affiliated with bank holding companies (BHCs). Figure source: Antoine Martin, Federal Reserve Bank of New York (2016).

was imposed on US dealer banks. The amount of cash financing obtained from bank-affiliated dealers by non-bank-affiliated dealers in this market declined by about 80 % from 2013 to the end of 2015. In that two-year period, a proxy measure of the effective bid-ask spread for US government securities repo intermediation shown in Figure 2.4 increased from under 4 basis points to about 16 basis points. In the last quarter of 2015, the three-month Treasury-secured repo rates paid by non-bank dealers were higher even than the three-month *unsecured* borrowing rates paid by banks (LIBOR), a clear and significant market distortion.

Another policy option would be a change in the application of the SLR to US government securities repo intermediation. For example, the measured amount of assets represented by government securities repo intermediation could be modified so as to recognize the effect of netting, whenever achieved safely within the same asset class. (The SLR rule already permits some netting of repo positions with the same counterparty, but not across counterparties.) An alternative would be to increase conventional risk-weighted capital requirements to the point that the SLR is not close to binding, as discussed in Chapter 1.

## 2.3 SLR degrades monetary-policy passthrough

Duffie and Krishnamurthy [60] show how the SLR also induces a pronounced increase in money-market rate dispersion at the end of each calendar quarter.[8] Table 2.1 provides statistics bearing on the end-of-quarter effects on money-market rates, based on a sample from January 1, 2015 to June 30, 2016. The table shows the mean value of each reported variable, excluding the end-of-quarter, as well as the change at the end-of-quarter, and the 95 % confidence interval around this change.

**Table 2.1:** End-of-quarter effects on selected money-market rates, for the period January 1, 2015 to June 30, 2016. Source: Duffie and Krishnamurthy [60].

| Variable | Mean, excluding quarter-end | Quarter-end change | 95 % confidence interval |
| --- | --- | --- | --- |
| Fed private-sector RRP volume | $94.2 bn | $206.1 bn | [170.6, 241.5] |
| 1-week T-bill rate – IOER | −26.3 bps | −6.7 bps | [−10.9, −2.5] |
| O/N TPR TSY repo – IOER | −19.4 bps | 0.0 bps | [−1.5, 2.2] |
| O/N GCF TSY repo – IOER | −6.4 bps | 26.4 bps | [21.0, 31.7] |
| O/N Non-Fin CP – IOER | −17.0 bps | −5.0 bps | [−7.0, −3.1] |

Table 2.1 shows that, during the sample period, take-up at the Fed's RRP facility rose by an average of $206.1 billion at the ends of quarters. We also see that the 1-week T-bill rate and the overnight non-financial commercial paper rate fell at quarter ends by between 5 and 7 basis points.[9] The movements in the 1-week T-bill rate imply that the overnight return on T-bills fell by about 47 basis points. The data also show that the GCF treasury repo rate rose on quarter ends by an average of 26 basis points, whereas the triparty repo rate was nearly unchanged. Finally, the table shows that all of these rates were on average below the interest rate offered to banks on their excess reserves (IOER), with the T-bill rate and the triparty repo rate the lowest, and the GCF repo rate the highest. In mid-2016, the GCF repo rate went well above IOER on quarter ends.

These effects are consistent with the heavy impact shown in Figure 2.6 of the leverage ratio rule on foreign-headquartered banks at the ends of calendar quarters. When banks scale back their balance sheets, they offer less repo financing because of the leverage ratio rule. The resulting contraction in lending in the GCF repo market drives up the GCF repo rate. At the same time, because banks scale back borrowing at quarter ends, cash investors that normally invest in bank deposits seek alternative cash investments. This explains the fall in the 1-week T-bill rate and the overnight non-financial

---

**8** This section is based in part on Duffie and Krishnamurthy [60].

**9** When interpreting the fall in the 1-week T-bill rate, one should keep in mind that the T-bill rate reverses and rises back to the average value the day after quarter-end.

Billions of dollars

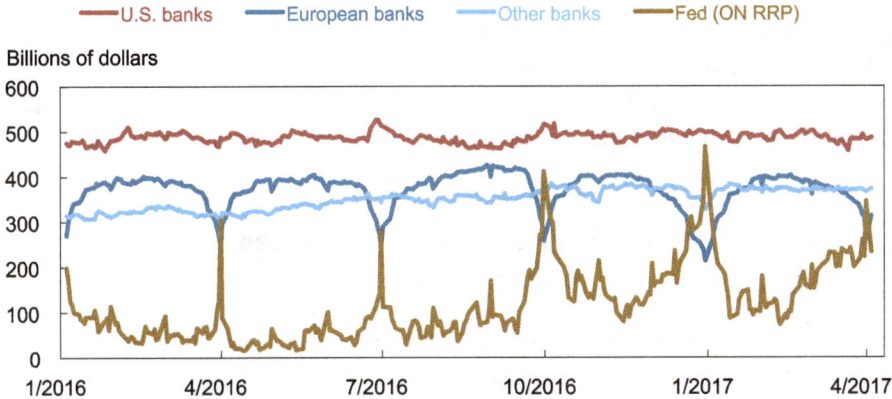

**Figure 2.6:** "European Banks Delever as Reporting Days Approach." Daily collateral outstanding in the triparty repo market and the Federal Reserve's overnight reverse repo (ON RRP) facility. Source: Egelhof, Martin, and Zinsmeister [65]. Notes: Banks headquartered in the euro area and Switzerland report leverage ratios as a snapshot of their value on the last day of each quarter, while their US counterparts report quarterly averages. Totals only include trades backed by Fedwire-eligible securities — that is, US Treasury and agency securities.

commercial paper rate, as well as the fact the triparty repo rate does not rise. Additionally, this quarter-end effect also induces cash investors to place additional funds at the Fed's RRP facility. Ruane [139] shows that the amount of quarter-end movement of funds into the Fed's RRP facility essentially offsets the amount of funds coming out of G-SIB triparty repo funding.[10]

Munyan [129] shows that the quarter-end reductions in bank balance sheets are most pronounced for foreign banks. Unlike US banks, foreign bank compliance with the leverage-ratio rule is monitored at the ends of quarters based on the intra-quarter month-end snap shots.[11] Figure 2.6 shows clear evidence of this effect. In addition to large quarter-end rate effects, Munyan [129] shows smaller but distinguishable end-of-month effects. The total amount of triparty repos outstanding for US banks does not decline significantly at quarter ends. The total of triparty repos for European banks declines markedly at quarter ends. The quarter-end gaps in the supply of repos from European banks was filled by additional use of the Federal Reserve's reverse repurchase facility (RRP).

Copeland, Duffie, and Yang [48] estimate that, controlling for a battery of effects related to market conditions, the broadest gauge of overnight Treasury repo rates, the Secured Overnight Financing Rate (SOFR), is elevated on quarter-end days by about

---

10 See the figure at the bottom of page 22 of Ruane [139].

11 See, for example, Ruane [139]. US banks, however, comply quarterly under the "eSLR" rule, based on daily averaging within each quarter for on-balance-sheet items and averaging off-balance-sheet items at month-ends within the quarter.

10 basis points. The predicted impact of quarter-end balance sheet constraints on the GCF general collateral Treasury repo rate is much larger, at about 26 basis points, consistent with the fact that repo assets in the GCF market are constrained by SLR, whereas repo liabilities in the triparty repo market do not count toward the SLR.

## 2.4 Repo crunches in 2019 and 2020: Not caused by balance-sheet constraints

During September 16 through 18, 2019, US Treasury repo markets suffered severe disruptions. On September 17, SOFR soared to 315 basis points above the interest rate by the Federal Reserve on central bank deposits (IOR). In an efficient market, SOFR and IOR should be approximately the same, by arbitrage reasoning, because both are interest rates for risk-free overnight investments available to banks. On September 17, interdealer Treasury repo rates, including the GCF general collateral rate, reached more than 700 basis points above IOR. A similar pattern was observed on March 17, 2020, when SOFR again spiked above IOR on news of the COVID-19 pandemic.[12]

These repo market crunches were not caused primarily by balance sheet constraints. Rather, as shown by Copeland, Duffie, and Yang [48], the main cause of these disruptions was a lack of sufficient central bank deposits, called "reserve balances," to meet the intraday payment timing demands of large dealer banks while also satisfying regulatory supervisors that these banks were meeting post-GFC regulatory liquidity requirements.[13]

Jamie Dimon, the Chairman and CEO of JP Morgan,[14] commented on the repo crunch of September 2019 during JP Morgan's third-quarter 2019 earnings call (https://www.jpmorganchase.com/corporate/investor-relations/document/3q19-earnings-transcript.pdf), when he responded to a question[15] about "everything that went on in the repo markets" during the September 2019 repo market disruption by saying

---

**12** SOFR exceeded IOR by 44 basis points on March 17, 2019. The Fed cured this problem relatively quickly by supplying more reserves [40, 140].

**13** The most relevant regulatory liquidity constraints include the supervisory liquidity tests of the Fed's Large Institution Supervision Coordinating Committee (LISCC), especially the Comprehensive Liquidity Analysis and Review (CLAR) [107], and the failure planning requirements for Resolution Liquidity Adequacy and Positioning (RLAP). See Pozsar [136] and Copeland et al. [48].

**14** Dimon's comments were covered by, for example, Bloomberg (https://www.bloomberg.com/news/articles/2019-10-15/jpmorgan-felt-barred-from-calming-repo-market-by-regulations).

**15** Glenn Schorr, analyst at Evercore, questioned Dimon as follows. "Curious your take on everything that went on in the repo markets during the quarter, and I would love it if you could put it in the context of maybe the fourth quarter of last year. If I remember correctly, you stepped in the fourth quarter, saw higher rates, threw money at it, made some more money, and it calmed the markets down. I'm curious what's different this quarter that did not happen, and curious if you think we need changes in the structure of the market to function better on a go-forward basis."

"... we have a checking account at the Fed with a certain amount of cash in it. Last year [2018] we had more cash than we needed for regulatory requirements. So when repo rates went up, we went from the checking account, which was paying IOR into repo. Obviously makes sense, you make more money. But now the cash in the account, which is still huge. It's $120 billion in the morning and goes down to $60 billion during the course of the day and back to $120 billion at the end of the day. That cash, we believe, is required under resolution and recovery and liquidity stress testing. And therefore, we could not redeploy it into repo market, which we would have been happy to do. And I think it's up to the regulators to decide they want to recalibrate the kind of liquidity they expect us to keep in that account. Again, I look at this as technical; a lot of reasons why those balances dropped to where they were. I think a lot of banks were in the same position, by the way. But I think the real issue, when you think about it, is what does that mean if we ever have bad markets? Because that's kind of hitting the red line in the Fed checking account, you're also going to hit a red line in LCR, like HQLA, which cannot redeployed either. So, to me, that will be the issue when the time comes. And it's not about JPMorgan. JPMorgan will be fine in any event. It's about how the regulators want to manage the system and who they want to intermediate when the time comes."

On September 17, the total balances of the 100 largest US banks (by reserve balances) reached a multi-year low of $1.06 trillion. Intraday payments of reserves to the ten banks most active in the repo market were significantly delayed, a sign of hoarding of reserves, as documented by Copeland, Duffie, and Yang [48]. The Fed reacted quickly [108] by adding large amounts of reserves, driving SOFR-IOR spreads back to moderately low levels.

However, as March 2020 approached, the reserve balances of the ten dealer banks most active in the repo market were again near their low September 2019 levels. On March 17, 2020, the time of day by which half of daily incoming payments to these dealer banks had arrived reached a multi-year high, 155 minutes later than average. The Fed was able to quickly cure the September 2019 and March 2020 repo crunches merely by supplying more reserves to the market.

Copeland, Duffie, and Yang [48] find that a spike in repo rates is much more likely on quarter ends and on days on which (i) payments to the largest repo active dealer banks are significantly delayed, (ii) there are large Treasury coupon security issuances, (iii) large repo-active dealers have low reserve balances, (iv) there are combinations of these effects. Only the quarter-end effects are primarily related to regulatory balance-sheet constraints. Effects (i)–(iv) reflect an insufficiency of reserve balances held by the most active repo intermediaries.

# 3 Funding Cost Frictions

This chapter discusses the impact of dealer funding cost frictions on market liquidity. Again, debt overhang is the driver. The impact on market liquidity can be large even in the absence of regulatory capital requirements. For expositional purposes, I use the common modeling concept known as "risk-neutral probabilities." The market value of an asset can be computed as the expected payoff of the asset using risk-neutral probabilities, discounted to present value at risk-free interest rates.

## 3.1 An illustrative example: T-bill investment

The following simple example from Andersen, Duffie, and Song [10] illustrates the effect of debt overhang caused by funding costs. A dealer purchases $100 face value of one-year Treasury bills and commits to hold them to maturity. Risk-free interest rates are, for simplicity of illustration, assumed to be zero. The dealer purchases the T-bills at their mid-market value, $100. The purchase is funded by issuing unsecured debt. This could be motivated by a desire to increase the dealer's regulatory measure of High Quality Liquid Assets (HQLA). The dealer has an unsecured one-year credit spread of 50 basis points. At the end of the year, the T-bills will pay $100 and the dealer will repay $100.50 on its financing. The dealer's shareholders will therefore suffer a net loss in one year, after financing costs, of $0.50. This loss will be borne by the dealer's shareholders only if the dealer survives. Assuming the dealer's one-year risk-neutral probability $p^*$ of survival (no default) is 0.99, the initial shareholder equity value of the dealer is thus reduced by $p^* \times 0.50 = 0.495$. As depicted in Figure 3.1, this funding cost to shareholders is a transfer in value to legacy creditors, who now have access to additional safe assets in the event of default.

Were it not for the HQLA requirement in this example, the dealer would not conduct this trade at the given pricing terms. The dealer's shareholders benefit from this trade only if the T-bills can be purchased at a price below $99.50. For market making applications, we later consider the minimum bid-offer spread that the dealer must apply for shareholders to break even. Roughly speaking, in order to overcome the debt-overhang wedge associated with funding the investment in a new trade, a dealer must earn an excess return that is proportional to its unsecured wholesale credit spread for the investment period. The constant of proportionality depends on the form of funding, whether equity, unsecured debt, or a blend. For unsecured debt financing, the proportionality constant is near one.

## 3.2 Post-crisis increases in dealer funding costs

While funding costs have long been informally considered an input to dealer trading decisions, they increased dramatically with the widening of bank credit spreads dur-

https://doi.org/10.1515/9783110673050-003

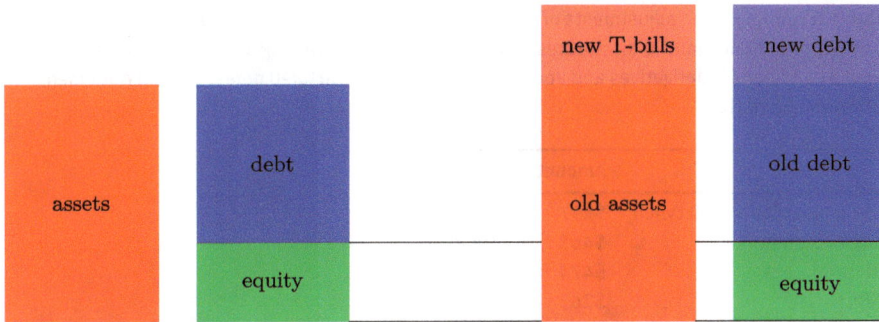

**Figure 3.1:** An illustrative example of debt overhang. A bank funds a purchase of Treasury bills by issuing debt of equal market value and equal maturity. At maturity, if the bank survives, the net return to shareholders is the yield on the Treasury bills net of the yield on the bank's debt, thus a loss equal to the yield spread of the bank's debt over the Treasury yield. If the bank defaults, the transaction has no impact on shareholders because of limited liability. The transaction should thus not be undertaken, from the viewpoint of shareholder value maximization, unless the Treasury bills can be purchased at a price that is sufficiently below the fair market value of the T-bills.

ing and after the GFC. As discussed in Chapter 1 and as shown Figures 1.4 and 1.5, post-GFC bank credit spreads are wide relative to their pre-GFC levels despite significantly increased capital levels. Berndt, Duffie, and Zhu [21] provide empirical evidence, controlling for bank riskiness and corporate debt risk premia, that this was caused by a post-GFC decline in the presumption by bank creditors that the largest banks are too big to fail. Beginning in 2011, major dealer banks started to formally account for their funding costs in the form of funding value adjustments (FVAs).[1] Some examples of disclosed FVAs are shown in Table 3.1.

As another example of the impact of increased funding costs, Wang, Wu, Yan, and Zhong [161] show that the "big bang" in the credit default swap (CDS) market in 2009 caused dealers to increase their bid-ask spreads on CDS in reaction to the increased funding costs associated with the introduction of upfront payments. Wang, Wu, Yan, and Zhong [161] write: "Intuitively, the upfront payment is an impediment to trading, and so reduces the market liquidity, leading to higher bid-ask spreads." They found that "for a CDS contract with a spread level of 300 basis points, at the average level of the Libor-OIS spread in our sample, 32 basis points, the upfront payment introduced by the CDS Big Bang increases the bid-ask spread by 1.5 basis points. This is a sizeable

---

**1** This change in accounting practice is described by Cameron [33], Becker [19], and Andersen, Duffie, and Song [10]. As noted by Andersen, Duffie, and Song [10], dealers have been inappropriately treating FVAs as reductions in the market values of their swap books rather than as transfers from equity values to debt values. Although financial accounting standards do not support FVA practice, large accounting firms have accepted FVA disclosures in dealers' financial statements. See, for example, Ernst and Young [68] and KPMG [120].

**Table 3.1:** Funding value adjustments of major dealers (millions). Source: supplementary notes of quarterly or annual financial disclosures. The $1.5 billion 2013 FVA of JP Morgan includes an FVA of about $1.1 billion for derivatives and about $400 million for structured notes. Source: Andersen, Duffie, and Song [10].

|                                | Amount   | Date Disclosed |
|--------------------------------|----------|----------------|
| Bank of America Merrill Lynch  | $497     | Q4 2014        |
| Morgan Stanley                 | $468     | Q4 2014        |
| Citi                           | $474     | Q4 2014        |
| HSBC                           | $263     | Q4 2014        |
| Royal Bank of Canada           | C$105    | Q4 2014        |
| UBS                            | Fr267    | Q3 2014        |
| Crédit Suisse                  | Fr279    | Q3 2014        |
| BNP Paribas                    | €166     | Q2 2014        |
| Crédit Agricole                | €167     | Q2 2014        |
| JP Morgan Chase                | $1,500   | Q4 2013        |
| Nomura                         | $98      | Q1 2014        |
| ANZ                            | AUD61    | Q4 2013        |
| Bank of Ireland                | €36      | Q4 2013        |
| Deutsche Bank                  | €364     | Q4 2012        |
| Royal Bank of Scotland         | $475     | Q4 2012        |
| Barclays                       | £101     | Q4 2012        |
| Lloyds Banking Group           | €143     | Q4 2012        |
| Goldman Sachs                  | Unknown  | Q4 2011        |

effect as the bid-ask spread in our sample has a mean of 9.6 basis points and median of 5.3 basis points."

The next section provides a model of the debt-overhang impact of funding costs on bank equity values and the resulting incentives for reduced market making. In the remainder of the chapter, I focus on the effect of increased dealer funding costs on the post-crisis violations of covered interest parity (CIP) documented by Du, Tepper, and Verdelan [53] and Rime, Schrimpf, and Syrstad [138]. For a dealer to benefit its shareholders by arbitraging a CIP violation, the FVA calculations imply that the CIP basis must exceed the dealer's credit spread, as a reasonable approximation of the associated debt overhang wedge on financial intermediation.

## 3.3 A model of dealer funding costs

I provide here a simplified version of the model of shareholder funding costs of Andersen, Duffie, and Song [10]. There is a finite number of states of the world. The one-period risk-free discount is $\delta = 1/R$, where $R$ is the gross risk-free rate of return.

By the definition of risk-neutral probabilities, the market value of an asset with a payoff of $Z$ is $\delta E^*(Z)$, where $E^*$ denotes expectation with respect to risk-neutral probabilities.[2] This formulation does not assume the absence of arbitrage. Indeed, it is critical for the viability of dealers that they can overcome debt overhang costs to their shareholders by violating the law of one price, buying assets at prices lower than those at which they sell them.

At time 1, the dealer's assets pay some random amount $A$ and its liabilities claim $L$, a positive constant. To avoid singularities, I assume that $P(A = L) = 0$ and that the probability of the default event $D = \{A < L\}$ is not zero.

The dealer is considering the purchase of an asset with a per-unit payoff of $Y \geq 0$. The per-unit marginal funding required to buy the asset is $u$. Our base case is that the dealer funds the trade with new unsecured debt. Later, I extend to the case of equity funding, whether or not required by regulation.

After financing a position of size $q$ by issuing new debt, the dealer's total assets are

$$\mathcal{A}(q) = A + qY$$

and its total liabilities are

$$\mathcal{L}(q) = L + u(R + s(q)),$$

where $s(q)$ denotes the credit spread on the new debt. The limit credit spread $\lim_{q \downarrow 0} s(q)$ on the newly issued debt is equal to the credit spread $S$ on the dealer's legacy debt.[3]

The marginal increase in the value of the firm's equity, per unit investment, is, by definition,

$$G = \left. \frac{\partial \delta E^*\left[(A + qY - L - u(R + s(q)))^+\right]}{\partial q} \right|_{q=0}.$$

Andersen, Duffie, and Song [10] calculate that this marginal increase in equity value is

$$G = p^* \pi - \delta \operatorname{cov}^*(1_D, Y) - \Phi, \tag{3.1}$$

---

**2** For the existence of risk-neutral probabilities, one can assume that the market valuation functional $V$ is linear, in that $V(\alpha X + \beta Y) = \alpha V(X) + \beta V(Y)$, for any asset payoffs $X$ and $Y$ and any scalars $\alpha$ and $\beta$, and that $V$ is increasing, in that whenever $X \geq Y$ and $X \neq Y$, we have $V(X) > V(Y)$. Unless markets are complete, the risk-neutral probabilities are not uniquely determined.

**3** This fact is shown by Andersen, Duffie, and Song [10], who provide the explicit calculation $S = E^*(\phi)R/(1 - E^*(\phi))$, for a fractional default loss to creditors in $\phi = 1_D(L - \kappa A)/L$, where $\kappa \in [0, 1)$ is the recovery fraction of assets in the event of default. The remaining fraction $1 - \kappa$ is a frictional default distress costs, which is permitted be zero.

where $p^* = 1 - P^*(D)$ is the risk-neutral survival probability, $\pi = \delta E^*(Y) - u$ is the marginal profit on the trade, and

$$\Phi = p^* \delta u S \tag{3.2}$$

is known as the funding value adjustment (FVA).

The second term of (3.1), $\delta \operatorname{cov}^*(1_D, Y)$, reflects the potential for asset substitution. Purchase of a risky asset that is negatively correlated with the dealer's default benefits the dealer's shareholders because they can "walk away" from losses at default and keep gains when surviving.[4]

For low interest rates and high dealer survival probabilities, $p^* \delta$ is near 1, so the FVA per unit of funding, $p^* \delta S$, is approximately equal to the dealer's one-period credit spread $S$. If the asset is risk-free, implying that $\operatorname{cov}^*(1_D, Y) = 0$, then to benefit its shareholders the dealer must purchase the asset at a profit $\pi$ per dollar of funding that exceeds the dealer's credit spread $S$. If the asset is risky, but has a payoff that is positively correlated with the dealer's default, in that $\operatorname{cov}^*(1_D, Y) > 0$, then the required profit on the trade must be even larger, because of the "negative" asset substitution effect.

This model does not consider the dealer's opportunity to re-use the funding that is released if the asset is sold before it matures. This benefit is bigger for higher-turnover dealing businesses. For example, suppose the required funding $u$ is released and re-used for an otherwise identical trade, $k$ times per period. Then, roughly speaking, the excess intermediation return that must be achieved on each asset purchase in order to overcome funding costs is reduced by a factor of $k$.

Consider for example the case of a safe asset, which we showed must be purchased so as to produce an excess return of approximately $S$ in a one-period model. With a dealer turnover rate of $k$ per period, the required excess intermediation return is reduced to $S/k$. This remains to be formalized with a proper multi-period model.[5]

## 3.4 CIP arbitrage could harm shareholders

I now summarize from Andersen, Duffie, and Song [10] an illustrative case study of the implications of funding value adjustments for the incentives of a dealer-bank to arbitrage violations of covered interest parity.

Du, Tepper, and Verdelan [53] and Rime, Schrimpf, and Syrstad [138] have shown that, since the GFC, the interest rates at which some big banks borrow US dollars outright in wholesale funding markets have usually been significantly below the rates for

---

4 Andersen, Duffie, and Song [10] calculate the second-order term in the Taylor series expansion of the shareholder gain in value, which also includes a natural and explicit asset-substitution effect.

5 This is a subject of ongoing research collaboration with Yao Zeng.

synthetic US dollar borrowing that could be obtained via foreign exchange (FX) markets. The synthetic method is to borrow a foreign currency, euros for example, and to exchange the euros for dollars (at spot, and back again at maturity) using FX forwards or cross-currency swaps. If the credit qualities of the two dollar positions, direct and synthetic, are the same, then the associated interest rates should be about the same, absent trade frictions, a point first noted by Keynes [117] and now known as covered interest parity (CIP). Any difference in these two rates, actual minus synthetic, is called the cross-currency basis.

Between 2010 and 2016, on average over major currencies, Du, Tepper, and Verdelan [53] estimate a cross-currency basis of about minus 24 basis points at 3 months and about minus 27 basis points at 5 years. Figure 3.2 shows violations of covered interest parity for G10 currencies at a maturity of five years. Violations of CIP in the Yen have been much wider, especially at quarter ends, as shown in Figure 3.3.

Rime, Schrimpf, and Syrstad [138] show that, once accounting for actual available transactions prices, profitable arbitrage of the cross-currency basis is possible for only a subset of highly capitalized banks. A more critical issue is whether CIP arbitrage is profitable to bank shareholders, whose profit is less than the profit to the bank's balance sheet, to the extent of the FVA.

For the purpose of a simple illustrative numerical example, suppose the one-year USD risk-free rate is zero. A bank considering a CIP arbitrage trade has a one-year credit spread of 35 basis points. The bank can thus borrow $100 with one-year USD commercial paper that promises investors $100.35. The bank could then invest $100 in one-year euro CP and swap the proceeds to dollars with a forward FX contract. In order to allow for an easy analysis of the attractiveness of this trading opportunity, we suppose that the resulting synthetic dollar asset has the same all-in credit quality as that of the bank's own commercial paper issuance, and that the two payoffs have no correlation under risk-neutral probabilities. We suppose that the synthetic dollar position promises $100.60, for a cross-currency basis of −25 basis points. The bank thus has a new liability with a market value of $100 and a new asset with a market value of $100.65/1.0035 ≈ $100.25, for a trade profit of approximately $0.25. However, the value of the trade to the bank's shareholders is negative because, conditional on the bank's survival, the expected incremental payoff to equity is $100.25 − $100.35 = −$0.10. Conditional on default, the bank's equity gets nothing. In order for this trade to benefit shareholders, the cross-currency basis would need to exceed the proportional funding cost of approximately 35 basis points.[6]

---

6 The value of this trade to dealer shareholders can also be computed directly, in this simple example, as the product of the risk-neutral survival probability and the expected trade net profit allocated to shareholders, after financing costs, conditional on the event of survival, which is 0.993 × ($100.60(0.993 + 0.0035) − $100.35) ≈ −$0.10.

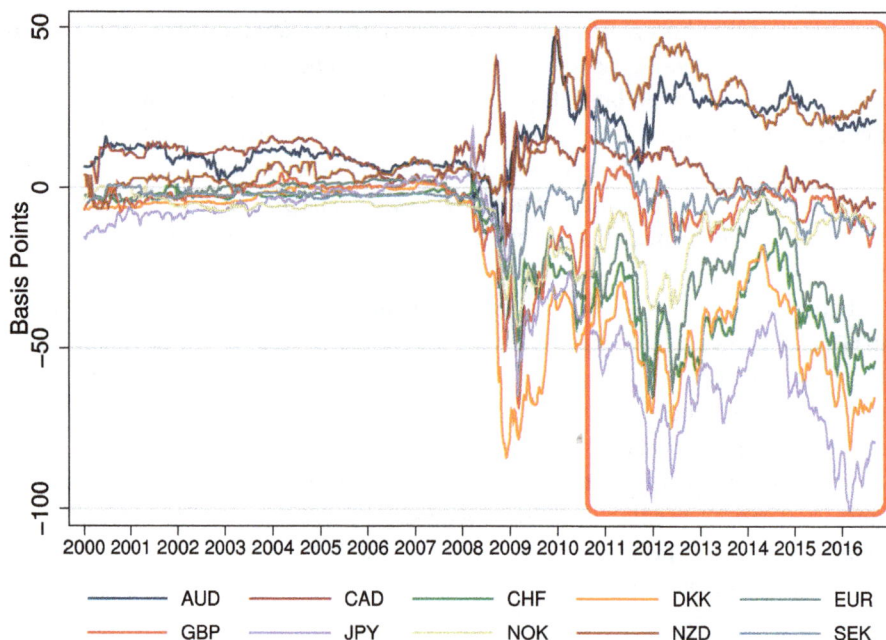

**Figure 3.2:** Ten-day moving averages of the five-year Libor cross-currency basis, in basis points, for G10 currencies relative to the US dollar. Source: Du, Tepper, and Verdelan [53].

Except at quarter ends, most or all of the effective CIP violations documented by Rime, Schrimpf, and Syrstad [138] have been below the associated proportional FVAs of global banks, based on current credit spreads.

As noted by Du, Tepper, and Verdelan [53], CIP violations were extremely small in the decade leading up to the GFC. Consistent with this, dealer-bank credit spreads (thus FVAs) were also much smaller before the GFC, as illustrated in Figures 1.3 and 1.4.

## 3.5 Regulatory capital and the cross-currency basis

Regulatory capital requirements pose an additional friction on CIP arbitrage that can be analyzed within the same modeling framework. Under the leverage-ratio rule, to pick one of the key regulatory-capital requirements, a bank with no capital headroom could meet its requirement by financing a fraction $C$ of an investment with new equity and the remaining fraction $1 - C$ with debt. In this case, based on the marginal value to shareholders of equity financing that is computed by Andersen, Duffie, and Song [10], the marginal cost of an asset to bank shareholders, per unit of funding, above that for all-debt financing, is

$$C(1 - p^* - \Phi), \tag{3.3}$$

where $\Phi$ is the FVA (3.2). For the largest US bank dealers, the supplementary leverage ratio rule implies that $C = 6\%$. From (3.3), the additional cost to the shareholders for the basis trade described in the above example is 2.1 basis points. When added to the FVA of about 35 basis points for unsecured debt funding, the total proportional debt-overhang cost to shareholders is approximately $35 + 2 = 37$ basis points.

This illustrative calculation ignores the additional balance-sheet cost to bank shareholders associated with the regulatory capital charge for the FX derivative, which could be roughly as large as that for the euro commercial paper. Funding the margin required for the FX derivative would also impose an FVA cost.

In practice, because of equity issuance costs, banks maintain slack in their regulatory capital constraints so that they do not need to obtain equity funding on a trade-by-trade basis. Allocations of regulatory capital usage are made to each trading desk on a periodic or ad-hoc basis. This can be complicated, especially because of cross-bank interaction effects involving several types of regulations.[7]

Assuming for simplicity a 50% loss given default on wholesale bank debt, we can replace $p^*$ in (3.3) with $1 - 2S$. The incremental cost for meeting the regulatory capital requirement, as an add-on to the FVA, is therefore roughly $CS$. Thus, for the purchase of safe assets, the shareholder breakeven excess intermediation return is the total annualized debt overhang cost to shareholders of roughly $(1 + C)S$. Notably, only a small fraction of this total cost to shareholders is caused by the regulatory capital requirement. Most of this cost is the FVA for debt financing.

Figure 3.3 from Du, Tepper, and Verdelan [53] shows that violations of covered interest parity for Japanese Yen spike dramatically at quarter ends, when regulatory capital is measured. This is consistent with an extremely rigid capital structure, that is, a high frictional cost to shareholders for raising capital in order to exploit CIP arbitrage at quarter ends.

---

7 According to Dimon [51], speaking of the regulatory constraints on JP Morgan, "We need to decide who we want to intermediate in the markets when there is stress. Several times in the last few years you have seen dislocation in our repo markets, Treasury markets and, in March 2020, all of our markets. In many cases, the Fed has had to step in to intermediate and help finance these markets. Part of the reason for this is the probably unintended confluence of new regulations. We now manage our bank to try to maximize and optimize across more than 20 capital and liquidity factors (we run the bank to serve customers, but we maximize capital and liquidity requirements for economic reasons). But the confluence of three main constraints (the LCR, the supplementary leverage ratio (SLR) rule and G-SIFI) created red lines that we cannot cross."

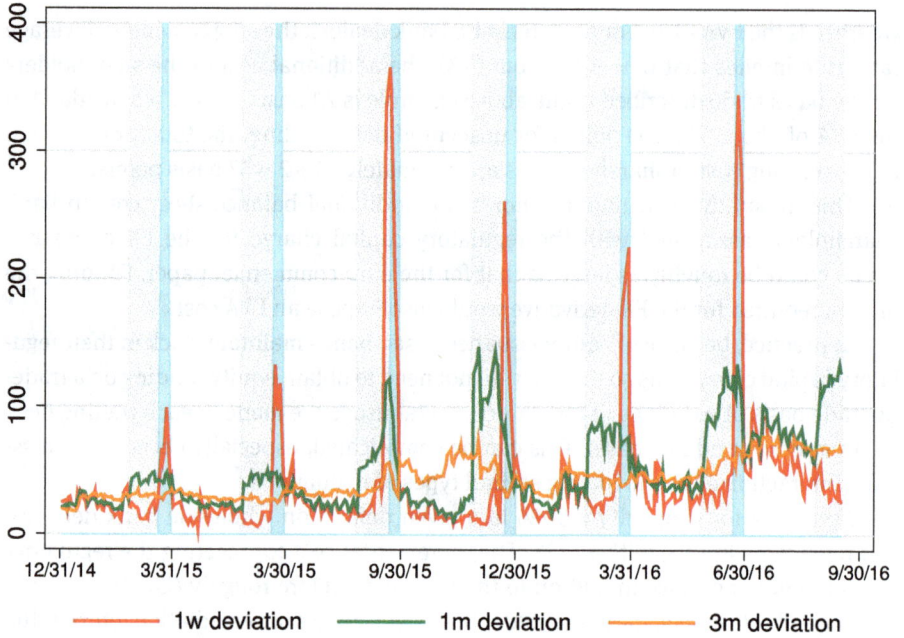

**Figure 3.3:** The absolute values of the one-week (red), one-month (green), and three-month (orange) Libor CIP basis for the Japanese Yen, relative to the US dollar. The blue and gray shaded regions correspond to periods during which the settlement and maturity of one-week contracts and one-month contracts, respectively, span the end of a quarterly reporting period. Source: Du, Tepper, and Verdelan [53].

# 4 Market Design Implications

This chapter[1] discusses how some of the market frictions caused by dealer debt over-hang and low competition in OTC markets can be mitigated by improvements in market design, without sacrificing financial stability.

Dealer intermediation practices have adapted to the higher post-GFC shadow prices for balance-sheet constraints. For example, as explained in Chapter 1, dealers are now more likely than pre-GFC to act as agents that match buyers and sellers, rather than as principals that buy or sell on their own accounts. Dealers have also made heavier use of financial market infrastructure, such as central clearing and "compression" services described later in this chapter, that eliminate redundant swap positions.

Under the US Dodd–Frank Act and the EU's Markets in Financial Instruments Directive II (MiFID II), regulators have mandated the use of multilateral trade platforms for some standard financial products. All-to-all trade, however, has been elusive, even for some heavily traded products like plain-vanilla swaps and government bonds. Despite the increased cost of access to dealer balance sheets, neither regulations nor market forces have had much success in increasing opportunities for buyside firms to trade directly with each other. Some OTC markets would become more efficient if some dealer intermediation is supplanted with all-to-all anonymous trade competition.[2] Here, the biggest deficiencies are related to a lack of price transparency and a weak degree of competitive bidding for trades. Policy objectives include deeper and more liquid markets, lower execution costs, and better allocative efficiency.

## 4.1 Opaque bilateral trade is inefficient

In an opaque bilateral over-the-counter (OTC) market, two buyside firms are rarely if ever be able to identify each other as sources of direct trading benefits. In OTC markets, a buyside firm often has no reasonable option but to trade with a dealer.

Bilateral (one-on-one) trade negotiation places a buyside firm at a bargaining disadvantage to a dealer. A buyside firm rarely has as much information as the dealer concerning the going price for the specific product. Thus, when offered given price terms by a dealer, a buyside firm cannot be confident whether the dealer's quotes are near the best available quotes in the market. The buyside firm does not know, moreover, which dealers are likely to provide the best quotes for the trade in question. Further, a buyside firm cannot force two or more dealers to compete effectively against each

---

1 Some portions of this chapter are based on Duffie [57].

2 I have a potential conflict on interest on this subject, having served as an expert in litigation in which dealers are alleged to have limited competition in OTC markets.

https://doi.org/10.1515/9783110673050-004

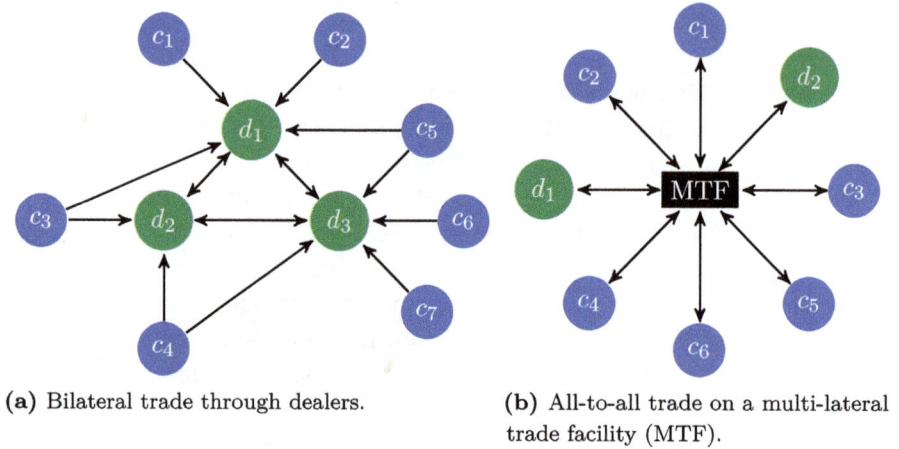

(a) Bilateral trade through dealers.

(b) All-to-all trade on a multi-lateral trade facility (MTF).

**Figure 4.1:** Schematics of markets based on (a) bilateral dealer-intermediated trade and (b) all-to-all trade on a multilateral trading facility (MTF) such as a central limit order book (CLOB).

other for the trade because of the bilateral nature of the bargaining encounter. I will now elaborate on this point.

A buyside firm has the option to reject the price terms quoted by the dealer with whom it is negotiating and then search for better terms from another dealer. In many cases, however, the buyside firm must negotiate with dealers sequentially, that is, one at a time. The buyside firm cannot choose the best from among various different dealers' simultaneously executable quotes. The mere fact that a buyside investor can eventually request quotes from different dealers does not in itself cause dealers to compete aggressively with each other in order to win the investor's trade. This situation is modeled by Zhu [163] and Duffie, Dworczak, and Zhu [62].

When facing a customer, each dealer holds a degree of monopoly power because the customer has no ability to pick the best of many simultaneously executable price quotes. The exercise of this market power reduces the volume of beneficial trade, raises search costs, and reduces matching efficiency [62].

## 4.2 Multilateral trade platforms

The distinction between bilateral customer-to-dealer trade and all-to-all trade on a multilateral trade facility is illustrated in Figure 4.1. A common multilateral trading method used in equity markets is a central limit order book (CLOB), onto which market participants can post limit orders or market orders. Market orders are for immediate execution against the best available limit orders. Limit orders remain on the order book until cancelled or until executed against a market order or a new crossing limit order. In practice, many variant types of orders are permitted.

Multilateral trade can be based on other trade protocols. For example, a request-for-quote (RFQ) protocol allows firms to launch a request to buy, or to sell, for a stated quantity. Authorized platform participants can respond with price quotes. The requester picks a quote. This is essentially an auction. Vogel [159] models the potential improvements associated with the introduction of multilateral trade platforms into an otherwise purely bilateral market. On some RFQ platforms, such as Brokertec's platform for European government securities, only dealers are permitted to provide quotes. Buyside firms can only request quotes.

On an all-to-all central limit order book, the best price quotes on the limit order book are transparent to all market participants and are simultaneously executable. For example, a buyer can choose the lowest of all of the simultaneously available quoted prices. This is the essence of effective pre-trade price transparency. Moreover, on an all-to-all CLOB, a buyside firm has the option to supply quotes to other market participants, thus offsetting some of its execution costs with the ability to both make and take quotes. Setting up a CLOB venue is justified if trading activity is sufficiently broad spread and frequent to generate profitable liquidity provision and to provide sufficient fee income to the venue operator. If trade activity is not sufficiently frequent, other all-to-all trade protocols can be effective. These include all-to-all RFQ and double-auction trading sessions at which multiple bidders post price-quantity pairs for purchase or sale. Each participant can post multiple bids. Demand and supply schedules constructed from the bids and offers, respectively, then determine a clearing price, at which orders to buy at higher prices are filled and orders to sell at lower prices are filled. (Orders at the clearing price may be rationed.)

## 4.3 Size discovery

Size-discovery trade protocols, such as workup and dark pools, are also popular. In this case, the trade price is fixed in advance of submissions of orders to buy or sell. A size-discovery market will not generally clear — there will either be an excess of buy orders or an excess of sell orders. The "heavy side" is rationed by some priority scheme, for example pro rata or in order of submission times.

Some size-discovery trade is designed to shield uninformed market participants from adverse selection by informed market participants and to limit front running.[3] Another motive is the ability to cross large and buy and sell orders without price impact, as modeled by Duffie and Zhu [61].

For example, Figure 4.2 illustrates the effect of introducing a workup trading session before trading begins on an exchange market. Without workup, unwanted inventory positions, whether long or short, decline slowly toward efficient levels, because investors trade gradually in order to mitigate price impact. With an initializing workup

---

**3** See Zhu [164] and Pancs [132].

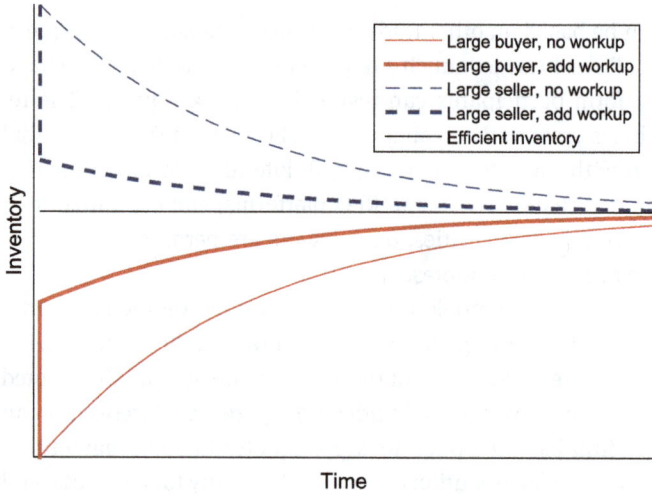

**Figure 4.2:** Inventory paths with and without a workup. The thin-line plots are the equilibrium inventory paths of a buyer and a seller in sequential-double-auction market. Plotted in bold are the equilibrium inventory paths of the same buyer and seller in a market with a workup followed by the same sequential-double-auction market. Figure source: Duffie and Zhu [61].

session, however, there is an opportunity for buyers and sellers to instantly cross large orders at a price that is frozen in advance of the expression of order sizes, thus insensitive to order sizes.

Antill and Duffie [11], however, show that the anticipation of future size-discovery sessions dilutes the incentive to trade on price-discovery platforms, such as the central limit order books of exchanges. Investors reduce the cost of their exchange price impacts by waiting for size-discovery sessions to unload large positions. As a result, exchange market depth declines. This decline in exchange market depth has the negative feedback effect of further discouraging the placement of orders on price-discovery exchanges, further reducing market depth, and so on. Size-discovery trading can therefore reduce the overall allocative efficiency of financial markets.

Degryse et al. [49] find that a one-standard-deviation increase in dark trading (including dark pools) for a particular stock is associated with a reduction in exchange market depth for that stock by 5.5 %. Nimalendran and Ray [131] find dark trading is associated with greater price impact in lit markets.

Consistent with these concerns about size discovery raised in theoretical and empirical research, the Markets in Financial Instruments Regulation (MiFIR - 600/2014/ EU) has placed caps on dark trading venues, so that[4] "the percentage of trading in a financial instrument carried out on a trading venue under those waivers shall be lim-

---

4 See http://eur-lex.europa.eu/legal-content/EN/TXT/?uri=uriserv:OJ.L_.2014.173.01.0084.01.ENG for the text of Regulation (EU) No 600/2014.

ited to 4 % of the total volume of trading in that financial instrument on all trading venues across the Union over the previous 12 months," and "overall Union trading in a financial instrument carried out under those waivers shall be limited to 8 % of the total volume of trading in that financial instrument on all trading venues across the Union over the previous 12 months."

Despite concerns about the impact of size discovery on allocative efficiency, size-discovery trade protocols are popular in some markets. For example, Fleming and Nguyen [76] find that approximately half of the volume of trade in the interdealer Treasury market is conducted in workup sessions. Collin-Dufresne, Junge, and Trolle [42] find that well over half of trade in credit default swap indices is conducted by size discovery, in the form of workup and matching sessions.

## 4.4 Multilateral trade facilities

In the US, Europe, and Japan, significant post-GFC regulations have improved pre-trade price transparency and competition, especially through mandated use of multilateral trade facilities (MTFs). Until new regulations forced some trading onto MTFs, most customer-to-dealer OTC trade was bilaterally negotiated between a buyside firm and a dealer.

In the first half of 2022, according to ISDA [112], more than 80 % of trade volume in standardized interest-rate swaps in the US was conducted on MTFs, which in the US are called swap execution facilities (SEFs). For each of the two most standardized credit default swap index products, over 95 % of trade volume was on SEFs.

Benchmark US Treasury securities are mainly traded between dealers on Brokertec, an MTF making heavy use of both CLOB and workup protocols. Trade between dealers and buyside firms in the US Treasury market, however, is negotiated bilaterally. Chapter 5 explains why this market structure was a major factor contributing to the dysfunctionality of US Treasury markets in March and April of 2020, following the declaration of the global COVID-19 pandemic.

In some markets, as depicted in Figure 4.3, buyside firms obtain their positions on customer-to-dealer MTFs at which more than one dealer can respond to a buyside firm's RFQ. In practice, it is rare for buyside firms to post their own quotes on an RFQ MTF. This narrowed use of MTFs represents a loss of efficiency because it reduces the degree of competition by dealers and lowers the efficiency of matching between buyers and sellers.

An additional reduction in the efficiency of OTC markets is associated with the fragmentation of trade in the same financial instrument across different MTFs. Fragmentation reduces competition and increases search costs.[5] The social costs of fragmentation of trade across MTFs is analogous, at a higher level, to the costs of dispersed

---

5 Chen and Duffie [35] show that fragmentation can actually improve the efficiency of all-to-all limit-order platform markets, because of the implications of strategic avoidance of price impact.

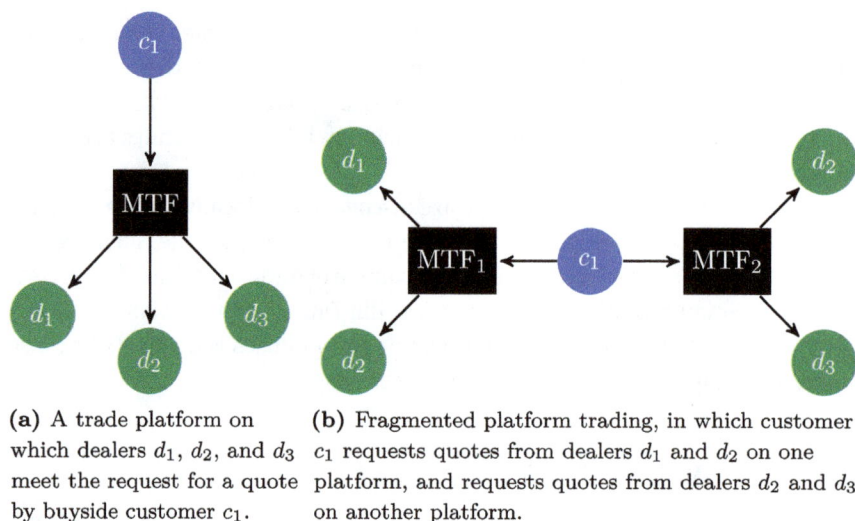

(a) A trade platform on which dealers $d_1$, $d_2$, and $d_3$ meet the request for a quote by buyside customer $c_1$.

(b) Fragmented platform trading, in which customer $c_1$ requests quotes from dealers $d_1$ and $d_2$ on one platform, and requests quotes from dealers $d_2$ and $d_3$ on another platform.

**Figure 4.3:** Fragmentation of trade across platforms is a limit on competition by dealers, and harms market liquidity.

bilateral trade. Colliard and Foucault [41] model a related cost of fragmentation across platforms. On the other hand, competition between MTFs may spur competition with respect to fees and technological innovation.

Figure 4.4, from a study of bond trading platforms by Hendershott and Madhavan [102], supports the theoretically anticipated relationship between the number of dealers providing quotes on Market Axess, a corporate bond MTF, and the expected trading cost to the quote requester, controlling for other factors. Figure 4.4 shows that expected trading costs decline rapidly with the number of dealers providing quotes on the same platform.

A significant fraction of interdealer trade is conducted on MTFs that use a central limit order book. The result, illustrated in Figure 4.5, is sometimes called a two-tiered market. In terms of improving competition and lowering trading costs to buyside market participants, post-GFC regulatory reforms fall short in many cases by failing to bring dealers and buyside firms together onto common venues using all-to-all anonymous trade protocols.

## 4.5 Post-trade price transparency

In any market format, competition is generally improved by fast and comprehensive post-trade transaction reporting. For example, beginning in 2003, the US brought post-trade price transparency into its corporate and municipal bond markets with the Transaction Reporting and Compliance Engine (TRACE). The quick public dissemination of transactions prices gives all market participants an indication of the prices

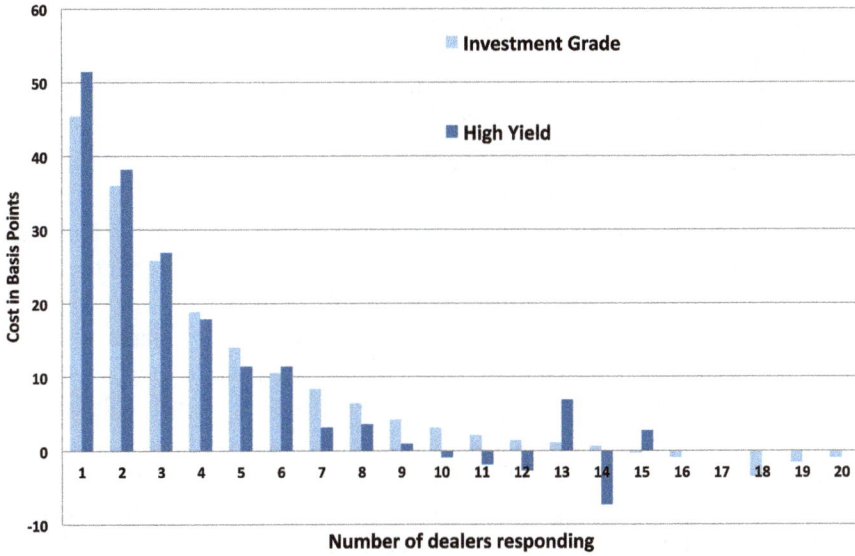

**Figure 4.4:** How transaction costs vary with the number of dealers responding to a request for quotes. Source: Hendershott and Madhavan [102]. The figure shows costs in basis points of notional amount, by the number of dealer responses in all electronic auctions on Market Axess in the sample with at least one response, broken down for investment-grade (IG) and high-yield (HY) bonds. Data are from January 2010 through April 2011, excluding all interdealer trades.

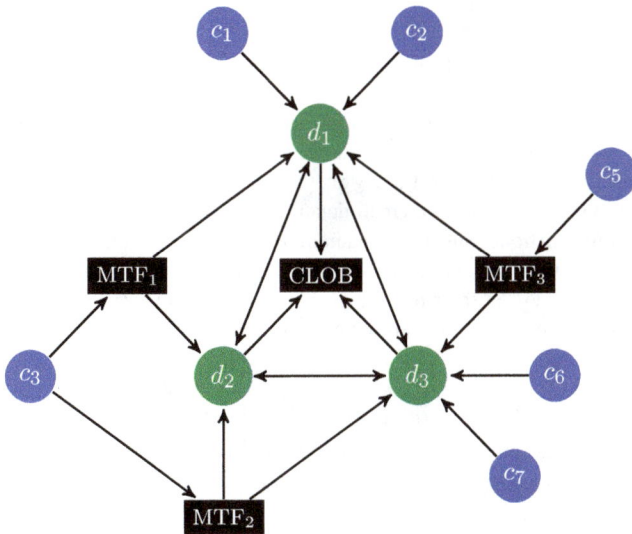

**Figure 4.5:** Now typical fragmented two-tiered OTC markets.

at which trades may be available in the next short interval of time. Knowledge of the going price is a particularly important mitigant of the bargaining disadvantage of buyside market participants, who generally have much fewer direct observations of trading encounters than do dealers.

The Dodd–Frank Act then aimed at the swap market. With some exceptions, standardized swaps have been designated for immediate and public transactions reporting. Japan followed a course similar to that of the US Europe's Markets in Financial Instruments Directive (MiFID II) and proposed MIFIR, implementing regulations that are more ambitious in scope than US trade-competition reforms.

As explained by Duffie, Dworczak, and Zhu [62], financial benchmarks are also a source of post-trade price transparency. The European Union has recognized the social benefits of reliable and transparent benchmarks with supporting legislation and regulation.

In addition to improving the ability of investors to shop for a better price, post-trade transaction reporting and published benchmark prices allows buyside investors to monitor and discipline dealers for the execution quality of their trades by comparing the prices that they obtained from a dealer with the prices at which other trades were conducted at around the same time. A dealer, aware of being monitored in this fashion, and at risk of losing reputation and repeat business over poor execution prices, will provide somewhat better pricing to its customers.

Turning to empirical evidence of the impact of post-trade price transparency on the liquidity and competitiveness of US corporate bond trading, Bessembinder and Maxwell [22] reported that

> The introduction of transaction price reporting for corporate bond trades through the TRACE system in 2002 comprised a major shock to this previously opaque market. Investors have benefited from the increased transparency through substantial reductions in the bid-ask spreads that they pay to bond dealers to complete trades. Conversely, bond dealers have experienced reductions in employment and compensation, and dealers' trading activities have moved toward alternate securities, including syndicated bank loans and credit default swaps. The primary complaint against TRACE, which is heard both from dealer firms and from their customers (the bond traders at investment houses and insurance companies), is that trading is more difficult as dealers are reluctant to carry inventory and no longer share the results of their research. In essence, the cost of trading corporate bonds decreased, but so did the quality and quantity of the services formerly provided by bond dealers.

This research also found that, with the introduction of TRACE, trade execution costs fell by about 50 % for those bonds whose transactions were covered by TRACE. Even for bonds not covered at that time by TRACE, transactions costs dropped by 20 %, perhaps because the prices of TRACE-reported bonds provide information on the market values of bonds that are not covered by TRACE.[6]

---

6 Edwards, Harris, and Piwowar [64] also find that TRACE reduced transactions costs, but Goldstein, Hotchkiss, and Sirri [89] find that less frequently traded bonds, and very large trades, showed no

Bessembinder and Maxwell [22] found a big increase in corporate bond trading volume on the electronic platform, MarketAxess, following the introduction of TRACE, writing, "We believe that TRACE improved the viability of the electronic market. In the presence of information asymmetries, less-informed traders will often be dissuaded from participating in a limit order market, knowing that their orders will tend to be 'picked off' by better-informed traders if the price is too aggressive, but left to languish if not aggressive enough. TRACE likely increased traders' willingness to submit electronic limit orders by allowing traders to choose limit prices with enhanced knowledge intradayof market conditions."

Going beyond bid-ask spread as a measure of trading costs, intraday price dispersion can be particularly informative of the role of search frictions that are exacerbated by low price transparency. In an opaque OTC market, the same bond, on the same day, can be traded by dealers at much different prices with some customers than with other customers, even if there has been no significant new fundamental information on the bond's quality during the day. Asquith, Covert, and Pathak [12] showed that the intraday dispersion of prices for riskier corporate bonds declined by over 40 % with the introduction of TRACE post-trade price transparency for those bonds. This represents a dramatic reduction in effective trading costs for many buyside investors.

Surprisingly, given the market-efficiency benefits of post-trade price transparency, TRACE transaction reports for US Treasury securities, which are available to regulators, are not released publicly, an issue revisited in Chapter 5.

## 4.6 Central clearing

Central clearing, among other benefits, reduces the need for dealer balance sheet space by netting the long and short positions of dealers at a central counterparty (CCP) [61]. The Dodd–Frank Act and MiFID II mandate that standard swaps are centrally cleared, subject to exemptions. Because of these post-GFC regulations, central clearing is now the norm in the swap market. For example, in the first half of 2022, over 89 % of US plain-vanilla interest rate swap transaction volume was centrally cleared. Over 97 % of volume in each the two most heavily traded dollar CDS index products was centrally cleared.[7]

---

significant reduction in bid-ask spread with the introduction of public transaction reporting under TRACE. Goldstein, Hotchkiss, and Sirri [89] and Asquith, Covert, and Pathak [12] do not find that TRACE increased trading activity. Indeed, Asquith, Covert, and Pathak [12] found that TRACE reduced trading activity significantly for high-yield bonds, perhaps because, with the reduced profitability of market making caused by greater price transparency, dealers had a reduced incentive to make markets, especially in thinly traded bonds.

**7** See ISDA [112].

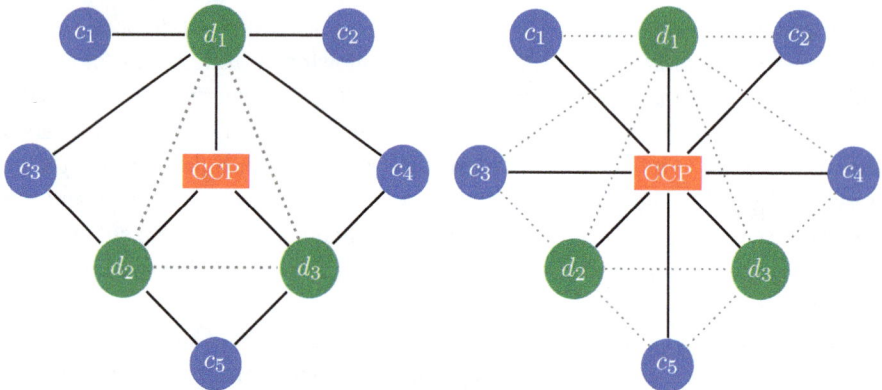

(a) A narrow interdealer CCP. Dealers $d_1$, $d_2$, and $d_3$ centrally clear their trades with each other. Positions of dealers with counterparties that are not clearing members, $c_1$, $c_2$, $c_3$, $c_4$, and $c_5$, remain on the balance sheets of dealers.

(b) Role of broad-market CCP. For example, the positions of $d_1$ with $c_1$, $c_2$, $c_3$, and $c_4$ can also be novated to the CCP, further reducing the balance sheet space of $d_1$ required to intermediate the repo market.

**Figure 4.6:** Original trades that were subsequently novated to the CCP are shown in dotted lines. Through this novation, known as "central clearing," the CCP becomes the buyer to each original seller, and the seller to each original buyer. With an interdealer central counterparty (CCP), as shown in Panel (a), a dealer such as $d_1$ novates to the CCP its trades with other dealer clearing members, $d_2$ and $d_3$, thus reducing its gross outstanding positions and use of balance sheet space, through the effect of netting long against short positions. This is also systemically safer (assuming the CCP is sound). Positions with counterparties that are not clearing members, such as $c_1$, $c_2$, $c_3$, and $c_4$, remain on the balance sheet of $d_1$. With a broad-market CCP, as shown in Panel (b), more positions can be novated to the CCP, thus further reducing the use of space on dealers' balance sheets. This mitigates the cost of intermediation to dealers' shareholders for meeting regulatory capital requirements, especially under the Supplementary Leverage Ratio Rule. Figure source: Duffie and Krishnamurthy [60].

US government securities transactions between primary dealers are centrally cleared by the Fixed Income Clearing Corporation (FICC).[8] As illustrated in Figure 4.6, a broad-market CCP would also clear the trades of PTFs and buyside firms, such as money market funds, pension funds, insurers, and hedge funds. This would allow more scope for long and short positions intermediated by dealers to be offset by netting at the CCP, thus reducing the use of dealer balance sheet space.[9] Again, the Supplementary Leverage Ratio (SLR) Rule discussed in Chapter 2 is especially implicated.

---

**8** Kahn and Olson [115] provide a breakdown of central clearing in this market. Baklanova, Dalton, and Tompaidis [14] outline the costs and benefits of central clearing in this market.

**9** Gerba and Katsoulis [84] provide evidence of the impact of capital regulations for the UK repo market.

The beneficial effects of multilateral trade platforms and CCPs are related, but are not the same. Multilateral trade platforms allow ultimate buyers and sellers to trade directly with each other, reducing the amount of dealer balance sheet space needed for the market to function. Broad-market CCPs increase netting after trades are executed, thus also reducing the need for space on dealer balance sheets. Broad-market central clearing, if done automatically and anonymously, also lowers barriers to the introduction of all-to-all trade because it encourages exchange operators to offer their trade services to a wide array of market participants who would otherwise need to clear their trades bilaterally with dealers.

One of the costs of wider use of central clearing in the Treasuries market is the increased cost of advance commitments to the CCP to provide financing the securities that would need to be held by a broad-market CCP in the event that one or more clearing members fail [148]. These commitments are currently provided by dealer clearing members, but could also in principle be provided by the central bank, as a lender of last resort.[10] Currently, non-dealers are not clearing members of the FICC, and seem unlikely to volunteer to become clearing members given the cost of liquidity commitment costs and the risk of losses that might occur at the default of other clearing members [148].

In 2017, however, a partial substitute for broad central clearing in the Treasury repo market emerged, when dealer banks began to have some of their positions with certain non-dealer counterparties, such as money market mutual funds, centrally cleared at FICC under a "sponsored repo" program.[11] This practice provided some relief, through netting, to regulatory capital constraints [6, 140]. Although the regulatory-capital reductions achieved through netting via sponsored repo is a benefit to market liquidity, this clearing model does not achieve the full benefits of central clearing, in that a sponsoring dealer remains ultimately responsible for the central clearing commitments of its sponsored customers, and the funds of the sponsored customer are not fully segregated at the CCP from those of the sponsoring dealer's funds.[12]

---

10 The Bank of England, according to its "Red Book" policy, stands ready to provide such financing to systemically important CCPs. The Fed, although authorized by Congress to do so under the Dodd–Frank Act, has not stated publicly whether it would actually provide this form of liquidity backstop to a CCP.

11 Kruttli, Monin, Petrasek, and Watugala [121] find that most hedge-fund repos are not centrally cleared.

12 Comotto [45] writes: "In sponsorship models, the dealer member has to make default fund and any similar contributions to the CCP on behalf of the client. The client is liable for variation margin and (except in the case of FICC) initial margin. However, in a Full Sponsorship Model, the dealer member also has to provide a back-up guarantee so that none of the default risk of the client is mutualized across the rest of the membership." "Because a sponsor has to make default fund contributions on behalf of a client and guarantee the client's settlement obligations to the CCP and any tail risk, the

For non-dealers in the Treasury cash securities market, the current approach to sponsored central clearing also involves a loss of anonymity and limits on the non-dealer's ability to trade with one dealer and have its trades centrally cleared through another [137].

## 4.7 Compression trading

Compression trading, a powerful method for conserving space on the balance sheets of major dealers, eliminates swap positions that are redundant from the viewpoint of their primary purpose of creating or offsetting exposures to market prices, but otherwise expose a dealer to counterparty risk. Along with the unnecessary counterparty risk, redundant swaps involve regulatory capital requirements and also increase the collateral requirements of dealers, both of which add to dealer balance sheet costs, as explained in Chapter 3.

Redundant long and short positions involving multiple dealers can be discovered via data-sharing arrangements between the dealers and special compression utilities, such as TriOptima. These compression utilities algorithmically initiate special trades between various pairs of dealers that effectively "tear up" the redundant swap positions, as illustrated in Figure 4.7. Substantial additional compression is achieved by

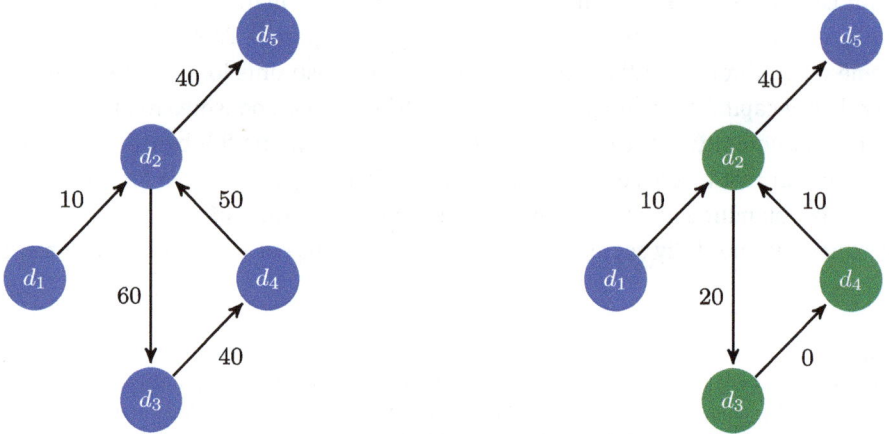

**Figure 4.7:** A compression trade that eliminates a redundant circle of positions of size 40 (counter-clockwise, involving dealers 2, 3, and 4) with a circle of clockwise trades of size 40. Counterparty exposures and initial margin are reduced without changing market exposures. Example service providers: TriOptima (over $1 quadrillion notional eliminated, largely interest-rate swaps).

---

Full Sponsorship model imposes significant costs on the sponsor that it must recover from the client or justify by achieving netting of the client's business. There is therefore a trade-off between the service cost of Full Sponsorship and its convenience for the client."

replacing the centrally cleared derivatives positions of clearing members with new positions that are virtually identical from the viewpoint of market risk, but that involve much lower gross notional commitments to the CCP. By 2018, TriOptima alone had triggered swap compression trades that tore up a total of over $1.1 quadrillion notional of swaps.

According to data collected and aggregated by the Bank for International Settlements (https://www.bis.org/publ/otc_hy1711.htm), the total gross market value of outstanding swap positions, before considering netting and collateral, has been dramatically reduced from pre-GFC levels, with no significant decline in the total annual volume of swap trade.[13] This total gross market value declined from approximately $35 trillion in 2009 to approximately $12 trillion as of December 2021, despite relatively stable overall transaction volumes over this period. I surmise that a significant portion of this improvement in the efficiency of balance-sheet usage is due to compression trading, under the heightened incentives for dealers to conserve balance sheet space that came with post-GFC capital requirements. Similarly, gross swap-market credit exposures, which adjust gross market values for legally enforceable bilateral netting agreements, but not for collateral, have fallen to their lowest level since 2007. For example, gross credit exposures declined from over $3.5 trillion at the end of 2012 to $2.5 trillion at December, 2021.

---

13 ISDA (https://www.isda.org/a/qVDDE/swaps-review-q4-2016.pdf) provides data on trading activity.

# 5 When the Fed Rescued the Treasury Market

When the World Health Organization declared in March 2020 that COVID-19 had become a global pandemic, investors around the world suddenly flooded dealers with demands to sell their Treasury securities. But the size of the US Treasury market had outstripped the capacity of dealers to intermediate the market under such stressed conditions, given the costs to their shareholders of reserving space on their balance sheets to hold larger and riskier asset inventories. The resulting episode of market dysfunctionality raises potential concerns over the safe-haven status of US Treasuries[1] and the cost to US taxpayers of financing growing federal deficits. Over the ensuring weeks, the Fed was able to largely restore market liquidity through its unprecedented rate of Treasury purchases and other actions, but the design of the Treasury market was revealed to be overdue for an upgrade.

This chapter[2] is a case study of the impact of post-GFC regulations on the functionality of financial markets. The case at hand is the US Treasury market and implications for improvements in its design. Policies that would improve market functionality, especially under stressed conditions like those of the Spring of 2020, include broader use of central clearing, post-trade transaction reporting with TRACE, a reduction of the Supplementary Leverage Ratio rule in favor of risk-based capital requirements, and an introduction of all-to-all trade.

---

**1** When issuing the US Treasury Department's 2016 "Notice Seeking Public Comment on the Evolution of the Treasury Market Structure," Antonio Weiss, Counselor to the Treasury Secretary, stated that "The Treasury market remains the deepest, most liquid market in the world, a source of safety and liquidity, and a haven in times of turbulence."

**2** This chapter relies in part on my Hutchins Center Working Paper [59], prepared for presentation on May 27, 2020, at the Brookings Institution meeting "COVID-19 and the financial system: How and why were financial markets disrupted?" I am grateful for comments from or conversations with Bill Allen, Sriya Anbil, Michael Bordo, John Cochrane, Dobrislav Dobrev, Michael Fleming, Guy Debelle, Andy Filardo, Michael Fleming, Jean-Sébastien Fontaine, Kenneth Garbade, Itay Goldstein, Beth Hammack, Bob Hall, Bob Hodrick, Jeffrey Ingber, Anil Kashyap, Frank Keane, Tim Geithner, Sven Klingler, Don Kohn, Arvind Krishnamurthy, Nellie Liang, Hanno Lustig, Antoine Martin, James McAndrews, Dennis McLaughlin, Bill Nelson, Gerard O'Reilly, Jun Pan, Patrick Parkinson, Elena Pastorino, Simon Potter, Hyun Shin, Manmohan Singh, Andreas Schrimpf, Jeremy Stein, Neal Stoughton, Vadimir Sushko, John Taylor, Ramin Toloui, Paul Tucker, Yesha Yadav, Joshua Younger, David Weisbrod, David Wessel, Haoxiang Zhu, and several anonymous market participants. Other summaries of the market dysfunctionality in government securities markets induced by the COVID-19 crisis include Barone, Chaboud, Copeland, Kavoussi, Keane, and Searls [16], Committee on Capital Markets Regulation [44], Financial Stability Board [73], Liang and Parkinson [122], Hauser [98], Joint Staff Report Inter-Agency Working Group for Treasury Market Surveillance [110], Board of Governors of the Federal Reserve System [26], Vissing-Jorgensen [158], Government Accounting Office [90], Fontaine, Garriott, Johal, Lee, and Uthemann [80], and Brainard [28].

https://doi.org/10.1515/9783110673050-005

## 5.1 Still a safe haven?

In response to the shocking news on March 12, 2020 of a COVID-19 global pandemic, investors sold huge quantities of Treasuries. The space available on dealer balance sheets for temporarily warehousing these trade flows diminished, bid-offer spreads widened dramatically, the yields of similar-maturity Treasuries were no longer close to each other, market depth plummeted, Treasury yields rose sharply, and settlement failures soared. The market for Treasuries was dysfunctional for several weeks.

In a massive response designed to shore up market liquidity, the Federal Reserve System purchased roughly $1 trillion of Treasuries in the three-week period from March 16, and then continued to buy at a high rate [83, 79, 85]. The Fed also offered unconstrained short-term financing for dealers' Treasury inventories. On April 1, the Fed temporarily exempted Treasuries and reserves from the Supplementary Leverage Ratio (SLR). By the end of April, these and other emergency actions by the Fed had significantly calmed the market.

Despite the success of the Fed's aggressive actions to restore liquidity to the Treasury market, the COVID-19 Crisis revealed the limited extent to which the secondary market for Treasuries can safely and efficiently handle surges in investor trading demands that can be expected, episodically, in coming years. Although the Fed accomplished what it needed to do, the lack of a robust private-market structure should not be acceptable based on the notion that the Fed can rescue the market as a last resort.

The bulk of trading of Treasuries initiated by non-dealer investors is intermediated by a small number of bank-affiliated securities dealers. Post-GFC regulatory reforms, however, have limited the appetite of these dealer-banks to warehouse investor flows on their balance sheets. New capital requirements and other new regulations[3] now force bank shareholders to bear far more of the costs of financing their market-making inventories. Although these rule changes improved financial stability and reduced implicit bailout subsidies to bank creditors, huge post-GFC federal deficits have caused the stock of marketable Treasuries to grow significantly, relative to dealer balance sheets, as shown in Figures 5.1 (large US bank dealers) and 5.2 (all primary dealers).

In short, the Treasury market has outgrown the capacity of dealers to safely intermediate the market on their own balance sheets, raising questions about the future safe-haven status of Treasuries and concerns over the cost to taxpayers of financing growing federal deficits.

In 2020 alone, the stock of marketable US Treasuries held in private hands increased from about $17 trillion to about $21 trillion. As shown in Figure 5.1, even after

---

**3** Beyond higher dealer capital requirements, increased dealer credit spreads induced by other post-crisis reforms imply higher debt funding costs for dealer inventories, as explained by Andersen, Duffie, and Song [10] and Berndt, Duffie, and Zhu [21]. Klingler and Sundaresan [119] analyze dealer balance sheet costs for Treasuries in their Appendix B.4.

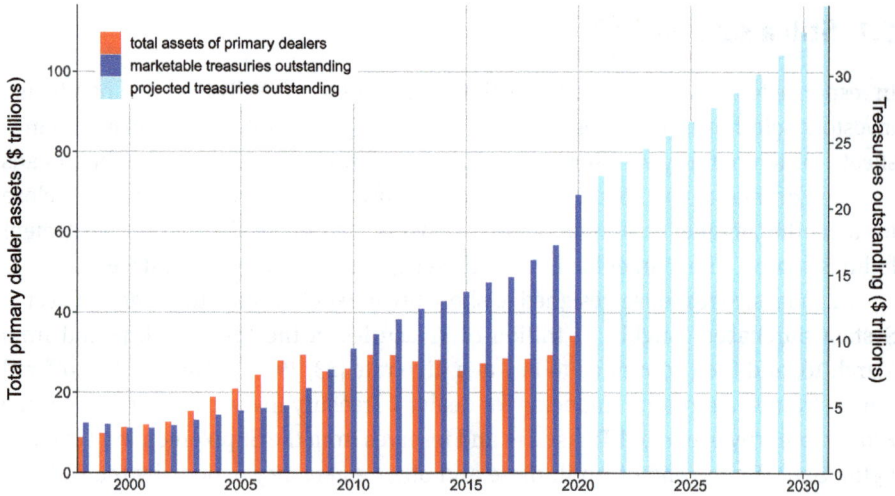

**Figure 5.1:** In blue (right vertical scale) are shown year-end total outstanding amounts of marketable Treasuries, 1998–2020 (data: FRED), with projections for 2021–2031 based on projections made on March 5, 2021 by the US Congressional Budget Office (https://www.cbo.gov/system/files/2021-03/56996-budget-outlook.pdf). In red (left vertical scale) are shown the total assets of the holding companies of the primary dealers designated by the Federal Reserve Bank of New York, year by year.

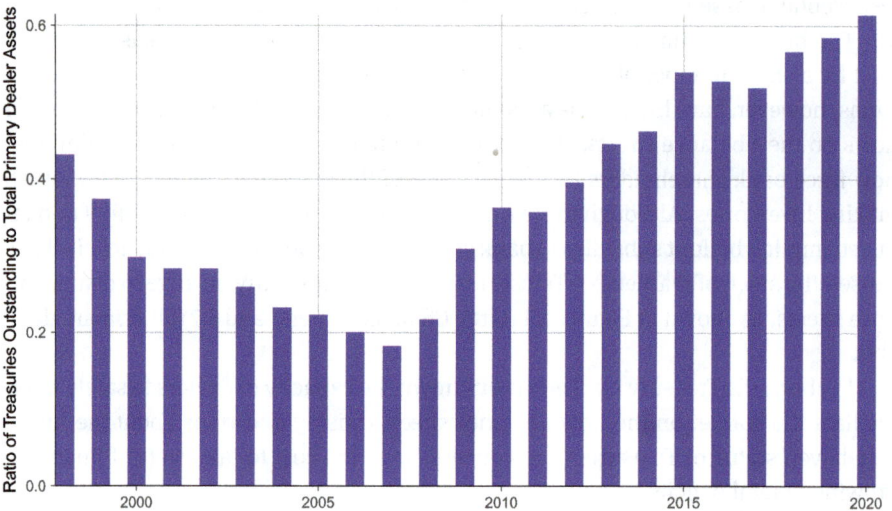

**Figure 5.2:** The ratio of Treasuries outstanding to total Fed primary dealer assets at the holding company level. Data: FRED and public corporate disclosures.

the immense fiscal responses of the US government to the COVID-19 Crisis in 2020 and 2021, the stock of Treasuries outstanding is projected to continue growing at a high rate. Extremely large projected fiscal deficits, relative to GDP, could also begin to increase Treasury yield volatility. According to Congressional Budget Office [46] projections in July 2022, the total amount of federal debt held by the public will rise from 96 % of GDP in 2023 to 185 % of GDP in 2052, far above the previous peak of 106 % of GDP in 1946. The stress on dealer balance sheets of handling future surges in trade demands could be magnified by increases in the volatility of Treasury prices. This involves an adverse feedback effect by which lower market depth causes yet greater price volatility.[4] Some European sovereign bond issuers suffered a nasty taste of this feedback in 2011–2012.

The secondary market for US Treasuries has two main segments.[5] In the customer-to-dealer segment, buyside investors trade with dealers. The buyside investors include hedge funds, pension funds, insurance firms, foreign central banks, sovereign wealth funds, operating companies (for cash management), mutual funds, and large multifunction asset management firms, among others. The second segment is the interdealer market, where dealers trade mainly with each other and principal trading firms (PTFs) [95]. The PTFs trade exclusively on electronic limit-order-book markets using high-frequency trading (HFT) strategies. Limit-order-book trade is exclusively for on-the-run securities. In the interdealer market, dealers trade on limit-order-book markets and also bilaterally, whether through interdealer brokers (IDBs) or directly with each other. Dealers frequently use the interdealer market to offset or hedge inventory imbalances arising from customer trades. IDBs match buyers and sellers, providing anonymity to each.

To effectively intermediate large expected future increases in Treasury trade volumes using the current market design, bank holding companies would need to substantially increase their capital commitments to Treasury market intermediation. Bank holding company shareholders, however, would not benefit from this commitment of capital unless intermediation rents, including bid-offer spreads, rise sufficiently. Even with higher bid-offer spreads, there would be episodes of extreme illiquidity and elevated yield volatility. In light of reduced secondary market liquidity, the issuance prices of Treasuries would be lower, raising the cost to US taxpayers of financing government spending.

Meanwhile, the risk of an accident in the plumbing of the Treasuries market, where trades are cleared and settled, already suggests the need for a more robust system of central clearing.[6] The central clearing of Treasuries trades by all large active investors would also significantly reduce the need to warehouse trade flows on

---

4 Eisenbach and Phelan [66] provide a model in which a safe asset market functions well if deep enough, but that the market can break down with prices falling precipitously if intermediated by dealers subject to balance sheet constraints.

5 Eren and Wooldridge [67] analyze the structural vulnerabilities of this market structure.

6 See Hubbard, Kohn, Goodman, Judge, Kashyap, Koijen, Masters, O'Connor, and Stein [105], Group of Thirty [92], and relevant reports [152, 153, 150, 151] of The Treasury Markets Practices Group (TMPG). The TMPG states at its web site (https://www.newyorkfed.org/tmpg) that "The TPMG is com-

dealer balance sheets. Dealers would be better able to net their buy and sell trades with central counterparties (CCPs), as explained in Chapter 4. Further, given broad access to a CCP, some Treasury transactions could flow directly across all-to-all trade venues from ultimate sellers to ultimate buyers without necessarily impinging on limited dealer balance sheet space. The transparency of the trade settlement process would improve and counterparty settlement risk would decline, improving financial stability. The leverage of Treasury positions, which is frequently not controlled by margins in the bilateral Treasury repo market, would be more regularly controlled by CCP margin requirements. Depending on the results of an effectiveness study, the most natural central-clearing mandate would likely cover both repo and cash-market trades, among other related types of transactions for which central clearing is now available at the Fixed Income Clearing Corporation (FICC).

A broad central clearing requirement would add setup costs, margin financing costs, and clearing fees. This would be unpopular [148]. When a firm centrally clears its trades, it is effectively insuring other market participants against its own default. In terms of incentives, the cost to a firm of central clearing is internalized, but the financial-stability externalities (benefits to others) are not internalized. However, the growing strains on the current market structure, especially with respect to dealer balance-sheet capacity, suggest that the expense of much broader central is likely justified. Regulators of Treasury markets may now wish to consider a cost-benefit analysis of a broad mandate for central clearing, similar in scope to central clearing rules for derivatives markets discussed in Chapter 4.

## 5.2 Treasury markets became dysfunctional

In March 2020, Treasury trading volumes, as shown in Figure 5.3, were roughly double normal. In order to intermediate between sellers and buyers, dealers needed to warehouse some of the flood of sales from global investors responding to worsening COVID news.[7] For example, some large hedge funds sold in reaction to risk limits and heavy margin calls [39].

---

posed of senior business managers and legal and compliance professionals from a variety of institutions – including securities dealers, banks, buy side firms, market utilities, and others and is sponsored by the Federal Reserve Bank of New York."

**7** Motivations for these sales are explained by Schrimpf, Shin, and Sushko [141], Cheng, Wessel, and Younger [37], and He, Nagel, and Song [100]. In March through May of 2020, according to TRACE data provided by FINRA, the aggregate volume of Treasury transactions was roughly balanced between the customer-to-dealer and interdealer segments of the market. FINRA combines ATS and interdealer transactions into a single reporting category that I treat as interdealer, given that the majority of ATS trade is not customer-to-dealer and there is essentially no customer-to-customer trade.

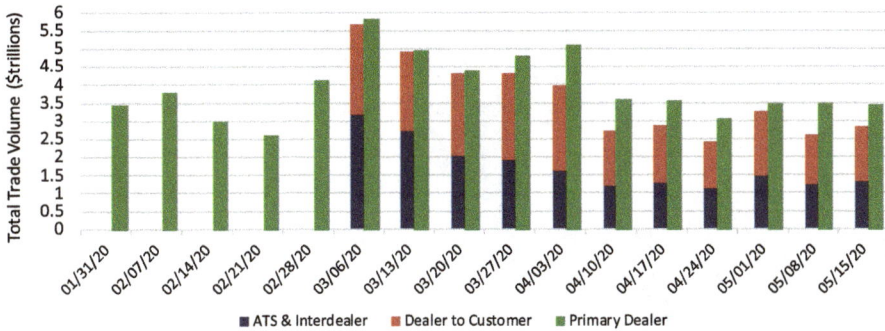

**Figure 5.3:** Total trading volume of US Treasury securities. In blue, from TRACE data, interdealer volumes (including ATS), for weeks ending on the indicated dates. In red, from TRACE data, dealer-to-customer volumes. In green, from FR 2004 data, primary dealer transactions for the week ending on the Wednesday before the indicated date. FR 2004 counts a single transaction between two primary dealers as two transactions, one for each dealer. TRACE data series are publicly accessible on a regular basis beginning only in March 2020. Data sources: TRACE data (https://www.finra.org/filing-reporting/trace/data/trace-treasury-aggregates) provided by FINRA. FR 2004 data (https://www.newyorkfed.org/markets/primarydealers) from the Federal Reserve Bank of New York.

Figure 5.4 shows that the March 2020 gross foreign sales of US Treasury notes and bonds to US residents (almost of whom would be US dealers) was an extreme outlier, about $700 billion above the previous all-time record high. Large foreign sellers included central banks managing their currency prices. In March 2020, according to the Treasury's International Capital Flow Report (https://ticdata.treasury.gov/Publish/tressect.txt), foreign holders sold, net of purchases, $299 billion of Treasury bonds and notes, also far above normal. Gross sales are an important gauge of pressure on dealer balance sheets because net sales do not reflect the balance sheet space that dealers need to hold inventories of specific securities over the period of time needed to find a buyer for each individual note or bond. A substantial fraction of foreign official sector sales were of off-the-run Treasuries, which take more time to be matched with buyers.

In its 2020 Financial Stability Report [25], the Fed wrote that "As investors sold less-liquid Treasury securities to obtain cash, dealers absorbed large amounts of these Treasury securities onto their balance sheets. It is possible that some dealers reached their capacity to absorb these sales, leading to a deterioration in Treasury market functioning."

Figure 5.5 illustrates the concepts at play.[8] At an efficient market equilibrium, unconstrained competitive dealers match supply and demand at point *a*, where the

---

[8] Goldberg [86] discusses the role of dealer balance sheet constraints in the Treasury market in March 2020, and more broadly. He, Nagel, and Song [100] offer a model of "inconvenience yields" associated with the SLR regulatory capital constraint on dealer balance sheets and "find that during the two

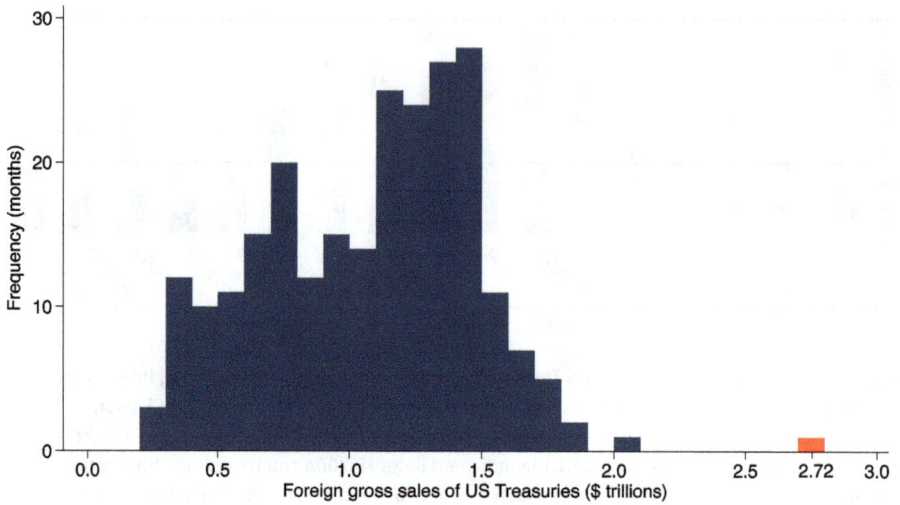

**Figure 5.4:** A histogram of monthly gross sales of US Treasury bonds and notes by foreigners to US residents, since January 2000. The gross-sales amount for March, 2020, indicated in red at $2.72 trillion, is the record high to date. Data source: US Department of the Treasury, Treasury International Capital System (https://ticdata.treasury.gov/Publish/s1_99996.txt).

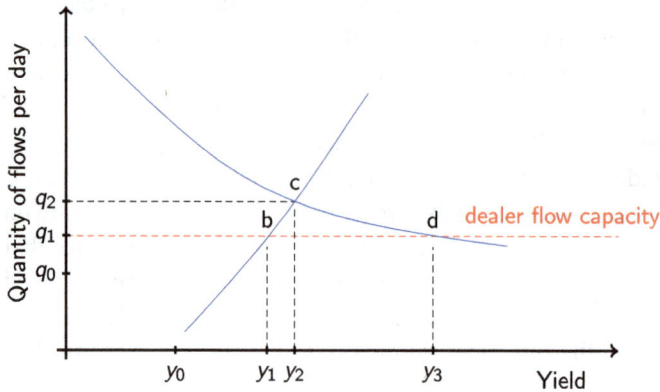

**Figure 5.5:** Supply and demand for liquidity under efficient and dealer-constrained market conditions.

quantity $q_0$ is traded at the yield $y_0$. When, however, the quantity of demands to trade is large enough, dealers can be constrained from matching flows at the efficient market equilibrium point $c$, at which $q_2$ would have been traded at yield $y_2$. Under dealer flow

weeks of turmoil, Treasury yields rose substantially above maturity-matched OIS rates, reflecting the inconvenience yield." Du, Hebert, and Li [54] provide theory and evidence of a change in the pricing of Treasuries caused by post-GFC capital constraints on dealers.

constraints, only $q_1$ is purchased by dealers at a high yield $y_3$ (point *d*) and $q_1$ is sold by dealers at the lower yield $y_1$ (point *b*). This assumes that, under binding balance-sheet constraints, all market power is held by dealers, who provide take-it-or-leave-it quotes. If some investors have a degree of market power, the bid-offer spread would be smaller than $y_3 - y_1$, but dealer balance sheet constraints would similarly reduce the gains from trade between ultimate investors. Dealers are effectively flow constrained by the limited space on their balance sheets available to temporarily warehouse some of the assets sold by investors, while arranging for other investors to purchase the assets.[9] On peak days in the Spring of 2020, total daily settlements of Treasuries trades reached about $1 trillion dollars [75], of which a significant quantity was off-the-runs, which require more time to be matched to ultimate buyers. With such high trade volumes, even if the average time that a position is held on the dealer's balance sheet is short, the result can be a "backup" of dealer inventories that has the effect of a flow constraint on dealer intermediation.

The flood of customer orders to liquidate Treasury positions was only one of a number of COVID-crisis-induced increases in the assets of the largest bank holding companies. Margin collateral held by bank dealers rose in response to increased price volatility in many markets. Corporate customers drew heavily on credit lines [47, 70]. In the short run at least, the balance sheet space available to some large dealers was tightly constrained, after considering the complexity of regulatory requirements, imperfections in a bank holding company's internal processes for allocation of capital and liquidity to its various businesses, and the aversion of managers to the risk of breaching their internal limits.

The enormous purchases of Treasuries by the Fed shown in Figure 5.6 did not free as much space on bank holding company balance sheets as one might have hoped because the Fed pays for these Treasuries with reserves, which the banking system must absorb. Although reserves (deposits at the Fed) are perfectly safe and liquid, they are subject to the Supplementary Leverage Ratio Rule (SLR). On April 1, the Fed temporarily exempted (https://www.federalreserve.gov/newsevents/pressreleases/bcreg20200401a.htm) both Treasuries and reserves from the SLR rule for bank holding companies, although it was not until the middle of May that the Fed, the Office of the Comptroller of the Currency, and the Federal Deposit Insurance Corporation adopted a similar SLR exemption for commercial bank subsidiaries (https://www.federalreserve.gov/newsevents/pressreleases/files/bcreg20200515a1.pdf). Treasuries held by bank-affiliated dealers remain subject to risk-based capital requirements, given their obvious re-pricing risk.[10] Beyond regulatory capital requirements, dealer banks also place limits on their total economic balance-sheet risk, for example using

---

**9** For a related theory, see An and Zheng [8].

**10** Breckenfelder and Ivashina [29] analyze the implications of bank leverage constraints on market liquidity during the COVID-19 crisis. The SLR exemptions expired on April 1, 2021.

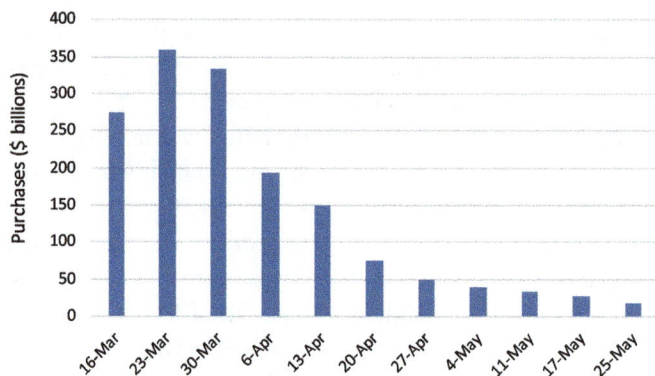

**Figure 5.6:** Total weekly purchases of Treasuries by the Fed from the week of March 16, 2020. Data: Federal Reserve.

metrics like Value at Risk that are often applied at the level of each trading desk, thus further dampening the incentives of dealers to absorb Treasuries with higher price volatility during March 2020 [149].

Bank shareholders are generally loath to issue new equity shares, especially in a crisis, given the expected adverse impact of issuances on share prices. In order to ensure that they can continue to meet a required ratio of capital to assets, bank executives therefore generally prefer to limit the growth of assets over the issuance of new equity, as reflected in Figure 5.1, which shows a dramatic post-2008 drop in the growth rate of assets of the largest US bank holding companies. When customers of their dealer subsidiaries are demanding liquidity and balance sheets are at the same time constrained by capital and liquidity ratios, dealers quote wider bid-offer spreads. Indeed, as shown in Figure 5.7, in March 2020 the bid-ask spreads offered by Treasury dealers to their customers increased by a multiple of over 10.

In the interdealer limit-order-book market for on-the-run 10-year Treasuries, market depth in March 2020 dropped by a factor of more than 10, as shown in Figure 5.8. New York Fed analyses by Fleming and Ruela [77] and Fleming [74] find similar losses in market depth and estimate that trade price impacts[11] increased above normal levels by a factor of over 5. Fleming [74] finds that bid-offer spreads in the interdealer market increased by a factor of about 5. PTFs did not significantly reduce their provision of liquidity to the interdealer Treasury limit-order book market, but most of the increase in trade volume had to be handled by dealers.[12]

---

**11** Price impact is the impact on market prices of net order flow. Fleming and Ruela [77] and Fleming [74] estimate price impact as the slope coefficient associated with a regression of one-minute price changes on net order flow (buyer-initiated trades less seller-initiated trades).

**12** According to JP Morgan analysis by Henry St. John, Joshua Younger, and Sejal Aggarwal, "Total depth at the top 20 levels on both sides of the market collapsed, with a fairly staggering peak-to-trough

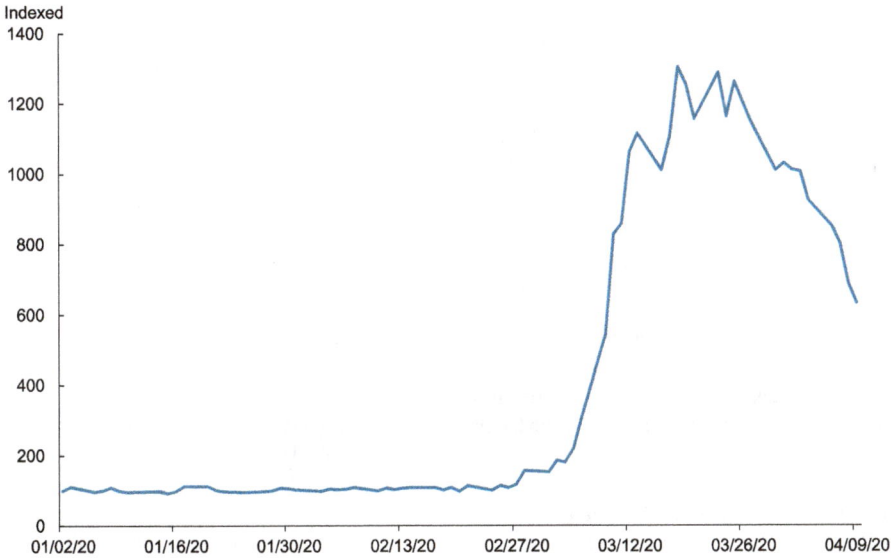

**Figure 5.7:** Treasury bid-offer spreads posted at Bloomberg, indexed to 100 at January 2, 2020. Figure source: Lorie Logan, Manager of the System Open Market Account and Head of the Open Market Trading Desk, Federal Reserve Bank of New York, published with her speech of April 14, 2020 (https://www.newyorkfed.org/newsevents/speeches/2020/log200414). The underlying data source is Bloomberg Financial LP.

The prices of Treasuries fluctuated wildly, compared to normal. As an example, consider the extreme hit to investors holding the 30-year Treasury bond, whose yield jumped from 1.34 % on March 16, 2020 to 1.77 % on March 18, 2020, representing a loss in market value of over 10 % in just two days.

At the beginning of March, yields were on average about 1 basis point out of alignment with a smooth yield curve, according a standard measure due to Hu, Pan, and Wang [103] that is now commonly known among practitioners as root mean squared error (RMSE).[13] By mid March, however, yields were over 3 basis points out of alignment, nearly triple the usual RMSE.[14] Off-the-run Treasuries, those not recently issued, were particularly mispriced, according to the Fed's 2020 Financial Stability Report [25]

---

decline of 92 %. The HFT fraction of this far larger slice of the order book similarly collapsed, falling to as low as 41 % in late March, from an average level of 88 % over the previous year." Source: "The Life Aquatic: Deeper Depth in the Treasury Market Infrastructure," JP Morgan Fixed Income Strategy, June 5, 2020.

**13** The Hu, Pan, and Wang [103] noise measure of Treasury market illiquidity is the square root of the mean squared error (RMSE) obtained when fitting the prices of Treasury securities to a smooth mathematical model of the yield curve.

**14** In its "US Treasury Daily" research report of May 21, 2020, JP Morgan reported that RMSE had declined from the high of 3.0 basis points to 1.3 basis points by the middle of May. In 2022, RMSE

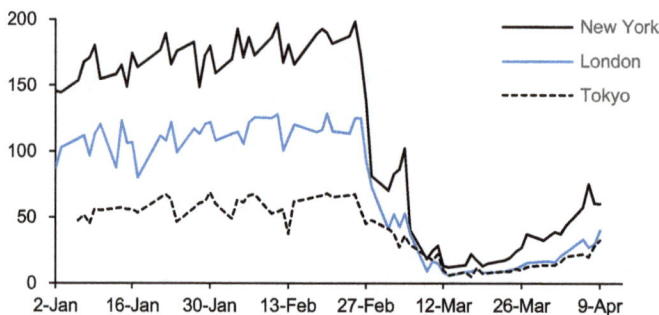

**Figure 5.8:** Treasury market depth on Brokertec for 10-year on-the-run notes. The market depth shown is the total of the quantities on the order book at the inside three price tiers on both sides of the limit order book, bid and ask, divided by two, in millions, for each of the New York, London, and Tokyo trade venues, respectively. The London data are averages for local trading until the New York open. The New York data are averages from the New York open to 3pm ET. The Tokyo data are averages for the local open to London open. The figure was obtained from JP Morgan and appeared in "Almost back to 'normal' An update on fixed income market liquidity," US Fixed Income Strategy, JP Morgan, Joshua Younger and Henry St. John, April 2, 2020. Fleming [74] finds a similar profile of declines in market depth.

and research reports of JP Morgan's Fixed Income Strategy Group. Normally, hedge funds and dealers would quickly step in to buy Treasuries whose prices are low relative to the prices implied by Treasuries that are close-maturity substitutes. Using data from 1990 to 2017, Goldberg [87] shows that the supply of liquidity by dealers to the US Treasury market goes down as RMSE rises, along with a decline in dealer gross positions.[15]

Similarly, the prices of Treasury derivatives went far out of alignment with the prices of the underlying deliverable Treasury notes [141, 17]. The cash-futures basis is the difference between the one-month repo rate for Treasuries and the corresponding repo rate that is implied by the prices of Treasury securities and Treasury futures contracts. In an efficient market, the actual repo rate and the implied repo rate should be nearly the same, as was the case in early 2020, given the opportunity available to hedge funds and dealers of arbitraging the basis between the two. In mid-March, however, the cash-futures basis grew to hundreds of basis points. Some large hedge funds that had previously taken cash-futures basis positions were caught off guard with highly levered positions in this trade. Hauser [97] comments that "Leverage rates of 40–60 times were common, but anecdotal reports suggest some ran much higher." The widening of the basis generated margin calls that forced large liquidations of ba-

---

again rose to abnormally high levels [149] and dealers noted substantial declines in liquidity in off-the-run Treasuries, according to the Federal Reserve Bank of New York [72].

**15** For the corporate bond market, Goldberg and Nozawa [88] liquidity supply by financially constrained intermediaries is a major determinant of market liquidity and prices.

sis trades,[16] further contributing to dislocations in Treasury prices and adding to the pressure on dealer balance-sheets.

Around the same time, traders were suddenly forced to work at home under COVID-19 social distancing requirements, an additional factor limiting dealer intermediation capacity. Yet the unusually large volumes handled by dealers, coupled with the choice of market-makers to ultimately quote exceptionally wide bid-offer spreads and minimal quantities at their best price quotes, seems to point more toward a high shadow price of access to over-stuffed balance sheets than to physical remote-site limits on traders.

With the Fed's exceptionally aggressive purchases of Treasuries, the exemption on April 1, 2020 of the SLR capital requirement for reserves and Treasuries, and the Fed's offer of essentially unlimited repo financing for dealer Treasury positions, Treasury market liquidity returned significantly toward normal by late April 2020 [25, 39].

March 2020 is perhaps the fourth time in the last century that the Fed rescued the US Treasury market from extreme dysfunctionality. Garbade [82] describes related episodes in 1939, 1958, and 1970. In September 1939, for example, stresses on the US Treasury market at the opening of the Second World War caused the Fed to "relieve" Treasury dealers of their positions, and then used the dealers as brokers, asking them to "bring to the Bank's attention the offerings of their customers."[17] Allen [7] describes how the Bank of England rescued the UK government securities market from bouts of illiquidity several times in the middle of the twentieth century.

It is natural for a central bank to provide support to its government securities market under such extreme circumstances. In this sense, the Fed's March 2020 rescue of the Treasury market was just one more case for the history books. Going forward, however, there is a counterproductive moral hazard in relying on future Fed rescues of the US Treasury market as an alternative to reforming the structure of the market so that it can better intermediate large episodic surges in demands for liquidity. Large surges

---

**16** For more details, see Hauser [97], Schrimpf, Shin, and Sushko [141] and Cheng, Wessel, and Younger [37].

**17** Garbade cites Federal Reserve Bank of New York (1940, pp. 26, 38, and 45–46), noting that "the dealers "were relieved of their positions by the Federal Reserve Bank of New York ... after the outbreak of war," that the New York Bank had "lightened the portfolios of the dealers and enlisted their services to submit to it all offerings made to them by customers." See also memo from Allan Sproul to files, Federal Reserve Bank of New York, September 1, 1939, noting that, at a dealer meeting at the New York Fed at 9:30 a.m. on September 1, Sproul stated that "it looked as if this might be the day," and that the Bank was 'prepared to see that no disorder develops ... In order to make our program effective, ...we are willing to clean up the dealers' net positions at a price 1/8 below last night's late closing prices." Two Fed rescues, also connected to military conflict, were in the summer of 1958, when US armed forces threatened to become involved in security concerns in the Middle East (Garbade, Chapter 15) and in May 1970, on the back of the announcement by President Nixon of a US military incursion from Vietnam into Cambodia and the subsequent tragic Kent-State protest (Garbade, Chapter 28). Kahn and Nguyen [114] provide additional historical context.

in trading demands under stress can be expected to arrive with greater frequency and magnitude, given the historically high and growing ratio of federal debt to GDP and the ballooning stock of outstanding Treasury securities relative to the capacity of dealer balance sheets.

## 5.3 Upgrading the US Treasury market with central clearing

As explained in Chapter 4, when a trade is centrally cleared, the original buyer and seller are no longer exposed to each other for settlement of the trade – they instead face the central counterparty (CCP). In case of a default, the surviving clearing members of the CCP are mutually responsible for providing the liquidity needed to resolve the failure, and to cover ultimate losses through capital contributions to the CCP. Typically, a CCP operator contributes a comparatively small amount of capital.

Treasuries transactions between primary dealers are centrally cleared at the Fixed Income Clearing Corporation (FICC). In the current market structure, transactions by PTFs in the interdealer market are not cleared by the CCP, but rather are cleared on the balance sheets of interdealer brokers. Customer-to-dealer Treasuries transactions are not centrally cleared. The Treasury Markets Practices Group [152] estimates that 12.7 % of US Treasury transactions are centrally cleared for both original counterparties, and that 19.4 % of transactions are centrally cleared between an interdealer broker and one of the original counterparties but not the other counterparty. The remaining 67.9 % of Treasuries transactions, most of which are customer-to-dealer, do not involve settlement at a CCP. Combining these estimates, a participant in the Treasuries market faces a CCP on only 22.4 % of Treasury transactions. By comparison, central clearing covers virtually 100 % of exchanged traded derivatives and equities, and the majority of swap-market transactions.

The left-hand schematic of Figure 4.6 illustrates the limited extent to which central clearing is currently applied in the US Treasury market, primarily by dealers and interdealer brokers that are members of the Fixed Income Clearing Corporation (FICC). The right-hand schematic illustrates a hypothetical CCP that could be used by dealers, interdealer brokers, PTFs, and other large investors that trade or repo Treasuries, such as pension funds, insurance firms, hedge funds, mutual funds, and other asset management firms.

Figure 5.9, from Fleming and Keane [75], shows a comparison between the actual daily settlement commitments of Treasuries dealers in the opening months of 2022 and the much smaller settlement commitments that would have applied in a counterfactual market with broad central clearing. Through the effect of netting purchases against sales, novation to the FICC of all commitments to settle cash Treasuries transactions would have reduced peak daily settlements by about 70 %, from about one trillion dollars to about $300 billion.

**Figure 5.9:** Total daily settlements of US Treasury securities transactions under the current market structure and in a counterfactual market structure with market-wide central clearing. Source: Fleming and Keane [75].

The general lack of central clearing in the US Treasury market is a significant missed opportunity to improve market robustness and efficiency, especially given the expectation of large future increases in risk flows in the Treasury market. Central clearing increases the transparency of settlement risk to regulators and market participants, and in particular allows the CCP to identify concentrated positions and crowded trades, adjusting margin requirements accordingly.

Central clearing also improves market safety by lowering exposure to settlement failures, which rose significantly during the most stressful days in March 2020,[18] as shown in Figure 5.10. As depicted, settlement failures rose less for trades that were centrally cleared by FICC than for all trades involving primary dealers. Central clearing reduces "daisy-chain" failures, by which firm A fails to deliver a security to firm B, causing firm B to fail to firm C, and so on. Fleming and Keane [75] find that broad central clearing would dramatically reduce settlement failures by cutting these daisy chains.

The existence of broadly accessible central clearing would also foster (although not on its own ensure) the emergence of trading directly between ultimate non-dealer

---

**18** Although settlement fails were relatively high in mid-March in comparison to surrounding recent months, fails were much below levels experienced during the financial crisis of 2008–2009, which preceded the implementation of settlement-fail penalties, as shown by Fleming, Keane, Martin, and McMorrow [78]. As explained by Ingber [109] in the context of GSCC, settlement fails can be converted by a CCP to future obligations. When the market is relatively weak at matching buyers and sellers, settlement fails can serve the useful purpose of expanding the "virtual supply" of Treasuries available for trade. An intermediary that does not have immediate access to a specific issue can nevertheless respond to a request for trade by selling the issue and then looking for the issue from others, sometimes failing to locate it. If settlement fails were stamped out, say with a much larger fail penalty rather than an improvement in market structure, dealers would often choose to decline counterparty requests for trade given taking the risk of a fail, which would eliminate some beneficial trades. See also Burne [32].

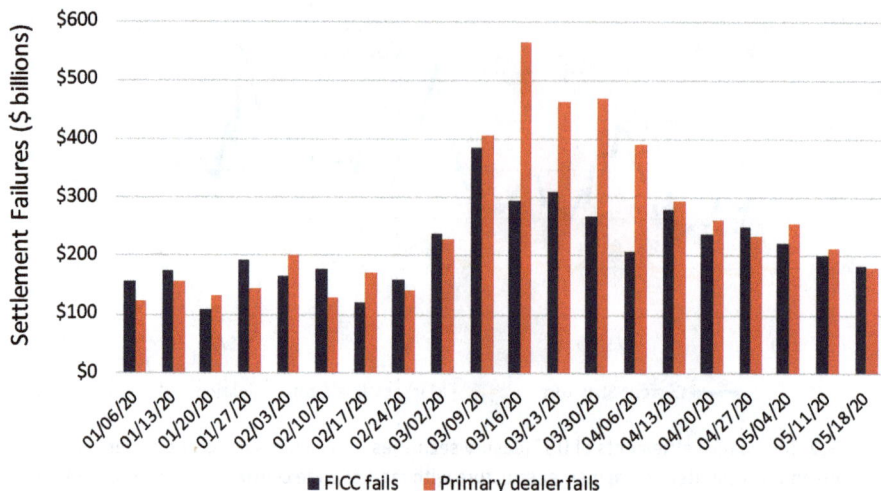

**Figure 5.10:** Treasuries settlement fails at FICC and for primary dealers. Data sources: FICC (https://www.dtcc.com/charts/daily-total-us-treasury-trade-fails) and Federal Reserve Bank of New York (https://www.newyorkfed.org/markets/gsds/search).

buyers and non-dealer sellers [58], further reducing the amount of dealer balance sheet space necessary to efficiently match buyers and sellers. All-to-all trade does not need to rely entirely on continuously operating limit-order-book markets. Trade in less actively traded off-the-run Treasuries can be conducted using all-to-all request-for-quote protocols. In a market that includes all-to-all trade, dealers would continue to play an important role in liquidity provision, especially for large trades, bilaterally and on trade platforms, just as dealers currently do in equities and derivatives markets.[19]

Central clearing also reduces the amount of dealer balance-sheet space necessary to maintain liquid markets. This arises from improved netting, by which a dealer's commitments to settle a buy trade with one counterparty and a sell trade with another can both be novated to the CCP, so that the dealer's settlement commitment and counterparty exposure is only the net of those of the buy and sell trades. To illustrate this concept with a simple example, suppose Firm $A$ is due to settle a purchase of $100 million of 10-year Treasury notes with Firm $B$. Meanwhile, $B$ is due to settle the purchase of $80 million of these Treasuries with Firm $C$, while $C$ is due to settle $90 million with $A$. The total of the settlement amounts at risk is thus $270 million. If, however, the three trades are centrally cleared at a CCP, the settlement risks collapse to $10 million for $A$ with the CCP, $20 million for $B$ with the CCP, and $10 million for $C$

---

**19** In 2022, the Securities and Exchange Commission [143] discussed reforms that may encourage all-to-all trade in US Treasuries. Pozmanter [135], DTCC [52], and Scott, Gulliver, Ondrejko, and Holt [142] discuss the benefits of broad central clearing in the US Treasury market.

with the CCP, for a new total amount of settlements of only $40 million. Ingber [109] provides realistic examples of netting and describes the improvements in netting resulting from the formation in 1986 of the Government Securities Clearing Corporation (GSCC), a precursor of FICC.[20]

In current accounting practice for the determination of US regulatory capital under the SLR requirement, commitments to settle a cash-market Treasuries transaction do not count toward assets, unless the settlement fails. This is not consistent with the regulatory capital accounting treatment for the closing leg of a Treasury repo, which is economically identical, but does count toward assets. Because of this accounting inconsistency, the shareholders of large dealer banks have an incentive for broader central clearing in the repo market, but this incentive does not apply to the market for cash Treasuries trading. Because broad central clearing in the cash market for Treasuries could also incite all-to-all trade, thus disintermediating some customer-to-dealer trade, it is unlikely to receive support from large dealers.

The Brattle Group [148] collected a range of views of market participants regarding the costs and benefits of central clearing in US Treasury markets. Among the concerns expressed in this survey is the risk of concentrating settlement at a central counterparty. A CCP like FICC is systemically important and, effectively, too big to fail. Because of these concerns, large US CCPs are designated by the Financial Stability Oversight Council (https://www.federalreserve.gov/paymentsystems/designated_fmu_about.htm) as systemically important, which implies a heightened level of supervision by US regulators. Without careful regulation, supervision, and failure resolution planning, CCPs can indeed present significant risks to financial stability [134]. These risks include high exposures to large clearing members, which also tend to be systemically important. Central clearing is an effective approach only with strong CCP risk management and regulatory oversight. Hubbard, Kohn, Goodman, Judge, Kashyap, Koijen, Masters, O'Connor, and Stein [105] and Group of Thirty [92] offer policy recommendations for the case of FICC.

The potential settlement risk to be centrally cleared for US Treasury securities trades is actually lower than that for equity trades that are already routinely centrally cleared. For example, Figure 5.11 shows that the total-market settlement risk for the 10-year Treasury note is typically lower than that for the SPDR S&P 500 ETF, a centrally cleared exchange-traded security. Shown in red is a rough estimate of the gross potential daily settlement risk for trades of the on-the-run 10-year Treasury note,[21]

---

**20** Chen, Chen, Ghosh, Pandey, and Walton [36] analyze the netting benefits of clearing in Canada's government securities market.

**21** This risk is the product of the dollar market value of total daily trading volume to be settled and an estimate of the one-day volatility of the return on the 10-year note, as implied by the market price of options on the 10-year note. Since the time at which I collected the implied volatility time series for the 10-year Treasury note, the CBOE has discontinued reporting these data.

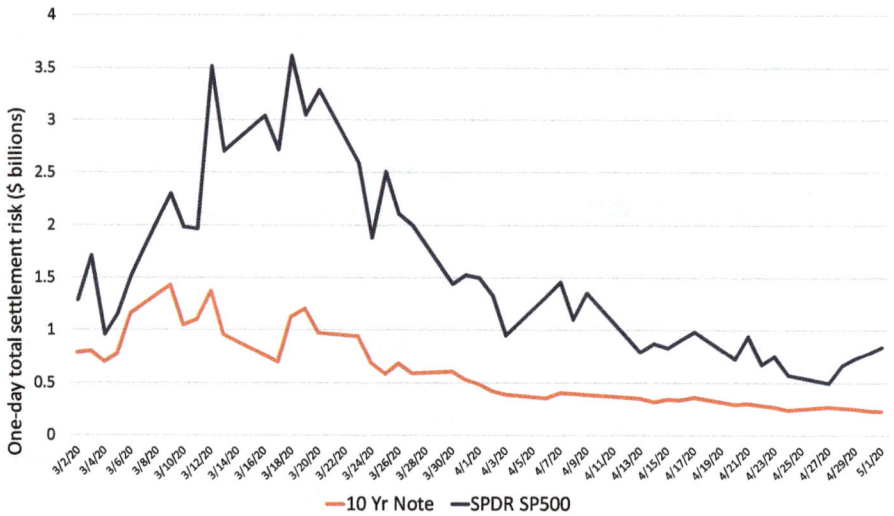

**Figure 5.11:** Estimated total one-day gross settlement risk for on-the-run 10-year US Treasury notes and for SPDR S&P 500 ETFs. One-day gross settlement risk is defined as the dollar market value of the volume of trade multiplied by the standard deviation ("volatility") of daily returns. Treasuries trades normally settle in one day (T+1), whereas exchange-traded equities such as the SPDR SP500 ETF settle in two days (T+2). Notional (principal amount) trade volumes for the 10-year Treasury note are weekly aggregates from TRACE data provided by FINRA (https://www.finra.org/filing-reporting/ trace/data/trace-treasury-aggregates). The weekly total of on-the-run trade 10-year notes (shown as on-the-run "> 7 years and <= 10 years") are divided by five to estimate average daily volume. The prices of the 10-year Treasury note were computed from yields reported by the US Treasury. SPDR S&P 500 ETF dollar volumes are based on share trade volumes and closing prices on NYSE-Arca, from data provided by Wall Street Journal (https://www.wsj.com/market-data/quotes/etf/SPY/historical- prices). The daily standard deviation of returns is approximated by dividing the reported annualized implied volatility of the Black–Scholes option-implied volatility by the square root of the number of trading days per year. The option-implied volatility for the S&P 500 and for the 10-year Treasury note are from data provided by the Chicago Board Options Exchange (CBOE).

based on all transactions in both the interdealer and customer-to-dealer market segments of the Treasury market, and incorporating the effect of daily price volatility. In blue, Figure 5.11 shows the larger estimated gross one-day settlement risk for the SPDR S&P500 ETF, which trades on NYSE Arca. The normal settlement cycle for equities is 2 days, as opposed to the one-day settlement cycle typical of Treasuries trades, so the difference in settlement risks illustrated in Figure 5.11 is actually understated. Like the vast majority of US exchange-traded equity transactions, transactions in SPDR ETFs are centrally cleared by the National Securities Clearing Corporation (https://www. dtcc.com/about/businesses-and-subsidiaries/nscc), which is designated as systemically important financial market infrastructure and regulated by the Securities and Exchange Commission (https://www.sec.gov/rules/sro/nscc-an/2015/34-76075.pdf).

Although the aggregate gross amount of settlement risk for typical US Treasury securities is no larger than that for some equities, the Treasury settlement commitments of individual investors can be extremely large, implying the need for significant commitments by clearing members to provide liquidity (financing) to the CCP in the event of the failure of one or more clearing members. For example, in the last quarter of 2019, there was a combined liquidity commitment by clearing members to the FICC's Capped Contingent Liquidity Facility (CCLF) of $108 billion, covering repos and cash trades of Treasury and Agency securities. Commitments by bank-affiliated dealers to the CCLF count against regulatory liquidity requirements, including the Liquidity Coverage Ratio (LCR). Increasing the breadth of central clearing of Treasuries transactions would substantially increase the liquidity commitments of clearing member firms to FICC. In addition to standing liquidity commitments, the amount of margin that must be posted to CCPs can grow markedly in stress periods, as Huang and Takáts [104] show was the case during the COVID19-induced stresses of March, 2020.

However, the current market approach of no central clearing for the majority of Treasuries (cash and repo) transactions does not remove the need for dealers to maintain large stocks of high-quality liquid assets and other sources of liquidity to cover margins and settlement risks for their bilateral Treasuries transactions. To the contrary, the netting of most purchases against sales at a CCP would lower the overall liquidity requirements of dealers, assuming that dealers continue to intermediate the market effectively. It would be difficult to estimate the amount of liquidity savings associated with central clearing without conducting a quantitative analysis of Treasuries transactions data.

Over the past decade, an expansion of central clearing in Treasury markets has been a subject of increasing policy discussion. In their 2015 "Joint Staff Report on the US Treasury Market (https://www.treasury.gov/press-center/press-releases/Documents/Joint_Staff_Report_Treasury_10-15-2015.pdf)," which addressed "significant and unexplained volatility" in Treasury markets that occurred on October 15, 2014, the staffs of the Treasury Department, Fed Board of Governors, the New York Fed, the SEC, and the CFTC wrote that the "significance of trading volume of firms outside the FICC membership – now larger in aggregate than that of FICC netting members – raises the question of whether trades cleared for non-CCP members are processed as prudently as those for firms inside the CCP. Trades cleared outside the CCP may not be subject to the same level of settlement risk mitigation techniques such as margin collection, disciplined clearing fund balance requirements, and pre-defined loss sharing arrangements."

In its 2017 Report to President Donald J. Trump on Core Principles for Regulating the United States Financial System (https://www.treasury.gov/press-center/press-releases/Documents/A-Financial-System-Capital-Markets-FINAL-FINAL.pdf), the Treasury Department addressed gaps in the central clearing of Treasuries, focusing only on the interdealer market, by writing: "First, there is less netting down of settlements than there would be if all interdealer market participants were FICC members. Second, if a large PTF with unsettled trading volumes were to fail, the failure could introduce risk to the market and market participants." The Treasury Department concluded its recommendations in this area by writing: "To better understand these arrangements and the consequences of reform options available in the clearing of Treasury securities, Treasury recommends further study of potential solutions by regulators and market participants."

In a 2017 hearing of the House Financial Services Committee reviewing the structure of US fixed-income markets (https://www.govinfo.gov/content/pkg/CHRG-115hhrg28749/pdf/CHRG-115hhrg28749.pdf), John Shay, Nasdaq's Global Head of Fixed Income and Commodities testified that "The clearing market structure, in our view, has fallen behind the realities of automated trading. The lack of a centralized clearing solution poses material counterparty risks to the market and leads to the following: less transparency as to the size of exposure; concentration risks; clients having to post collateral at multiple venues; and a decentralized default management process that is cumbersome and prone to delays and errors."

In a separate written submission to this hearing, Murray Pozmanter, Managing Director of DTCC (parent of FICC) and Head of Clearing Agency Services stated that "clearing of Treasury securities would provide several benefits, including the reduction of aggregate counterparty and credit risk in the system; increased transparency; more efficient use of collateral; and increased balance sheet relief for CCP members."

In its 2019 report, "Best Practice Guidance on Clearing and Settlement," the private-sector Treasury Markets Practice Group summarized its position on the "potential role for expanded central clearing in mitigating clearing and settlement risk," writing:

> The TMPG learned through its work that the changes to market structure that have occurred have also resulted in a substantial increase, in both absolute and percentage terms, in the number of trades that clear bilaterally rather than through a central counterparty. This principally stems from the increased prevalence of PTF activity on IDB platforms. The majority of dealer-to-customer activity also continues to be bilaterally cleared. Mandatory central clearing has long been required in the futures market, and under Dodd–Frank central clearing has now been mandated or incentivized for many swap instruments. Central clearing offers certain immediate benefits for individual firms, including transfer of counterparty credit risk to the CCP through novation, multilateral netting of exposures, and other risk mitigation features, such as margining, that also serve to reduce liquidity risks and risks to broader market functioning. However, these need to be weighed against other considerations such as the cost of clearing, the ability to access a CCP, and the concentration risk typically associated with central clearing. Members of the TMPG did not form a consensus view as to whether increased use of central clearing services should effectively be compelled, through either a regulatory mandate or strong regulatory incentives, but there was agreement that certain market participants were less likely to voluntarily move to more widespread use of central clearing in the current environment. Thus, the TMPG believes that to the extent that public policy interests are served by moving to more widespread utilization of central clearing, that is something best addressed by the official sector.

Broad central clearing would likely achieve significant balance-sheet economies and operational efficiencies by incorporating the central clearing of when-issued transactions,[22] Treasury auction settlements, and repo transactions, as was eventually done at GSCC [109].

Some of the benefits of central clearing could in principle be achieved through more rapid trade settlement, potentially even intraday settlement, although this would require new approaches to financing in the Treasuries market, which relies on the one-day settlement cycle to set up necessary financing.

## 5.4 Summary of lessons learned

Although significant reforms to the structure of the US Treasury market had long been discussed by the US official sector,[23] the weak functionality of the secondary market for US Treasuries that was revealed during the COVID-19 Crisis was a wake-up call. Given the enormous volumes of trade in this market, which will rise markedly with the massive upcoming growth in US federal debt, regulators of the US Treasury market may now wish to introduce major reforms that would improve financial stability, increase market transparency, and reduce the current heavy reliance of the market on the limited space available on dealer balance sheets for intermediating trade flows. This upgrade of the Treasury market would be a significant undertaking. Yet similarly onerous major upgrades of US financial market design and regulation were accomplished after the financial crisis of 2008–2009, which revealed important weaknesses in the markets for repos and swaps. For example, in the triparty repo market, dangerous intraday credit exposures in excess of $1.5 trillion were significantly reduced by a private sector task force (https://www.newyorkfed.org/tripartyrepo) empaneled by the Federal Reserve Bank of New York. In the swap market, the Commodity Futures Trading Commission implemented Dodd–Frank legislation that mandated broad central clearing of approximately $100 trillion in notional outstanding US dollar interest rate derivatives, according to ISDA (https://www.isda.org/a/CicTE/Key-Trends-in-the-Size-and-Composition-of-OTC-Derivatives-Markets-1H-2019.pdf). This reform has not damaged the liquidity or depth of the swap market – just the opposite.

---

**22** The when-issued trading of Treasuries, in the week before issuance, heightens settlement risk because of the longer delay between trade and settlement.

**23** See, for example, US Department of the Treasury and Federal Reserve [156], US Department of the Treasury, Board of Governors of the Federal Reserve System, Federal Reserve Bank of New York, US Securities and Exchange Commission, and US Commodity Futures Trading Commission [157], US Department of the Treasury [155], Adrian, Fleming, Goldberg, Lewis, Natalucci, and Wu [3]. The most recent broad discussion of reforms by the Inter-Agency Working Group for Treasury Market Surveillance [110] was triggered by the market dysfunction shown in March 2020.

In summary, key reforms to the regulation and structure US Treasury markets, so that they may function more effectively under stressed conditions among other benefits, include:

1. Broadening the requirement of central clearing of Treasuries transactions well beyond the transactions of primary dealers.
2. Encouraging the development of all-to-all trade, for example by removing exemptions for Treasuries platform markets from SEC regulations ATS and SCI.[24]
3. Restructuring bank capital regulations so that the SLR is not typically binding.[25]
4. Improving post-trade price transparency with the real-time publication of TRACE Treasuries transactions data that are already available to regulators.[26]
5. Establishing a standing Fed repo facility that provides Fed financing to investors who might prefer to finance some of their Treasuries, under stress, rather than sell them. Such a facility was actually instituted in June, 2021, although Group of Thirty [92] and Hubbard, Kohn, Goodman, Judge, Kashyap, Koijen, Masters, O'Connor, and Stein [105] recommend broadening access to this facility.[27]

---

**24** In January 2022, the Securities and Exchange Commission [143] proposed a new definition of "exchange" that would have the effect of covering the principal interdealer and multidealer-to-client platforms for Treasury securities and therefore require them to comply with Regulations ATS and SCI. Group of Thirty [92] and Group of Thirty [93] explain the implications.

**25** See a formulation for reliance on risk-based capital requirements in Chapter 1 that is consistent with a system-wide version of the SLR. See also the discussion by Group of Thirty [92], and Hubbard, Kohn, Goodman, Judge, Kashyap, Koijen, Masters, O'Connor, and Stein [105], who specifically recommend: "Permanently exclude reserves from the Supplementary Leverage Requirement (SLR) or consider adopting the global leverage capital standard for global systemically important banks (GSIBs) that would more likely serve as a backstop consistent with regulatory intent; Consider a countercyclical component of the SLR to be released in stress; Adjust the GSIB calculations, to (i) exclude reserves from the size measure, (ii) use average rather than quarter-end balance-sheet measures, (iii) reduce the cliff effect of moving to the next GSIB bucket, (iv) revalue the impact of the fixed coefficient component to adjust for economic growth and inflation, to avoid the GSIB surcharge from becoming unnecessarily constraining as banks grow along with the economy; Review treatment of short-term wholesale funding within the GSIB calculation, which unduly penalizes Treasuries and Treasury repo and may reduce bank dealers' flexibility to offer repo financing during stress; Review the ways in which overlapping liquidity regulations and their interaction with leverage capital calculations affect the willingness of dealers to make markets in Treasury securities and intermediate in Treasury repo markets, especially during stress, and assess whether those regulations could be simplified or made more flexible without adversely affecting the ability of banks to meet funding outflows in stress circumstances or in resolution."

**26** See Chapter 4, Group of Thirty [92], and Group of Thirty [93].

**27** FIMA (https://www.federalreserve.gov/monetarypolicy/fima-repo-facility-faqs.htm) was also established as a special repo facility that allows foreign monetary authorities with a custodial account at the Federal Reserve Bank of New York to obtain repo financing for the securities held they holds in their custodial accounts.

The efficiency and stability of the market for US Treasuries are public goods on which many market participants depend, without necessarily having the individual incentives to support. This is a matter of US national economic security because the Treasuries market is the instrument by which the US Government funds itself and is the foundation of the reserve-currency status of the US dollar. The US official sector now has a key role to play in reforming this market.

# Bibliography

[1]   Anat Admati, Peter DeMarzo, Martin Hellwig, and Paul Pfleiderer. The leverage ratchet effect. *Journal of Finance*, 73:145–198, 2018.

[2]   Tobias Adrian, Emanuel Moench, and Hyun Shin. Macro risk premium and intermediary balance sheet quantities. *IMF Economic Review*, 58:179–207, 2011.

[3]   Tobias Adrian, Michael Fleming, Jonathan Goldberg, Morgan Lewis, Fabio M. Natalucci, and Jason J. Wu. Dealer balance sheet capacity and market liquidity during the 2013 selloff in fixed income markets. FEDS Notes. Washington: Board of Governors of the Federal Reserve System, available at https://www.federalreserve.gov/econresdata/notes/feds-notes/2013/dealer-balance-sheet-capacity-and-market-liquidity-during-the-2013-selloff-in-fixed-income-markets-20131016.html, October 2013.

[4]   Tobias Adrian, Erkko Etula, and Tyler Muir. Financial intermediaries and the cross-section of asset returns. *Journal of Finance*, 89:2557–2596, 2014.

[5]   Tobias Adrian, Michael Fleming, Or Shachar, and Erik Vogt. Market liquidity after the financial crisis. *Annual Review of Financial Economics*, 9:43–83, November 2017.

[6]   Gara Afonso, Marco Cipriani, Adam Copeland, Anna Kovner, Gabriele La Spada, and Antoine Martin. The market events of mid-September 2019, available at https://www.newyorkfed.org/medialibrary/media/research/staff_reports/sr918.pdf. Staff report 918, Federal Reserve Bank of New York, March, 2020.

[7]   William A. Allen. *The Bank of England and the Government Debt Operations in the Gilt-Edged Market, 1928–1972*. Cambridge University Press, October 2019.

[8]   Yu An and Zeyu Zheng. Immediacy provision and matchmaking. *Management Science*, published online at https://doi.org/10.1287/mnsc.2022.4355, March 2022.

[9]   Sriya Anbil, Alyssa Anderson, and Zeynep Senyuz. Are repo markets fragile? Evidence from September 2019. FEDS working paper, available at https://www.federalreserve.gov/econres/feds/files/2021028pap.pdf, April 2021.

[10]  Leif Andersen, Darrell Duffie, and Yang Song. Funding value adjustments. *Journal of Finance*, 74(1):145–192, 2019.

[11]  Samuel Antill and Darrell Duffie. Augmenting markets with mechanisms. *The Review of Economic Studies*, 88(4):1665–1719, 2021.

[12]  Paul Asquith, Thomas Covert, and Parag Pathak. The effect of mandatory transparency in financial market design: Evidence from the corporate bond market. Working paper, National Bureau of Economic Research, available at https://www.nber.org/papers/w19417, April 2019.

[13]  Andrew Atkeson, Adrien d'Avernasz, Andrea Eisfeldt, and Pierre-Olivier Weill. Government guarantees and the valuation of American banks. *NBER Macroeconomics Annual*, 33:81–145, 2019.

[14]  Viktoria Baklanova, Ocean Dalton, and Stathis Tompaidis. Benefits and risks of central clearing in the repo market. Office of Financial Research Brief, available at https://www.financialresearch.gov/briefs/files/OFRBr_2017_04_CCP-for-Repos.pdf, March 2017.

[15]  Jack Bao, Maureen O'Hara, and Xing (Alex) Zhou. The Volcker Rule and corporate bond market making in times of stress. *Journal of Financial Economics*, 130(1):95–113, 2018.

[16]  Jordan Barone, Alain Chaboud, Adam Copeland, Cullen Kavoussi, Frank Keane, and Seth Searls. The global dash for cash: Why sovereign bond market functioning varied across jurisdictions in March 2020. Federal Reserve Bank of New York Staff Report, available at https://www.newyorkfed.org/medialibrary/media/research/staff_reports/sr1010.pdf, March 2022.

[17]  Daniel Barth and Jay Kahn. Basis trades and Treasury market liquidity. Office of Financial Research Brief, available at https://www.financialresearch.gov/briefs/files/OFRBr_2020_01_Basis-Trades.pdf, July 2020.

https://doi.org/10.1515/9783110673050-006

[18]  Basel Committee on Banking Supervision. Revised Basel III leverage ratio framework and disclosure requirements. Consultative document, Basel Committee on Banking Supervision, available at https://www.bis.org/publ/bcbs251.pdf, June 2013.

[19]  Lukas Becker. BAML and Morgan Stanley take FVA losses. *Risk*, available at http://www.risk.net/risk-magazine/news/2390522/baml-takes-usd497-million-fva-loss, February 2015.

[20]  Antje Berndt, Darrell Duffie, and Yichao Zhu. Across-the-curve credit spread indices. Technical report, Stanford Graduate School of Business, available at https://papers.ssrn.com/sol3/papers.cfm?abstract_id=3662770, July 2020.

[21]  Antje Berndt, Darrell Duffie, and Yichao Zhu. The decline of too big to fail. Working paper, Graduate School of Business, Stanford University, available at https://papers.ssrn.com/sol3/papers.cfm?abstract_id=3497897, June 2022.

[22]  Hendrik Bessembinder and William Maxwell. Markets: Transparency and the corporate bond market. *Journal of Economic Perspectives*, 22:217–234, 2008.

[23]  Hendrik Bessembinder, Stacey Jacobsen, William Maxwell, and Kumar Venkataraman. Capital commitment and illiquidity in corporate bonds. *Journal of Finance*, 73(4):1615–1661, 2018.

[24]  Board of Governors of the Federal Reserve System. Capital planning at large bank holding companies: Supervisory expectations and range of current practice. Board of Governors of the Federal Reserve System, Washington DC, available at https://www.federalreserve.gov/bankinforeg/bcreg20130819a1.pdf, August 2013.

[25]  Board of Governors of the Federal Reserve System. Financial stability report. Washington DC, Federal Reserve System, available at https://www.federalreserve.gov/publications/files/financial-stability-report-20200515.pdf, May 2020.

[26]  Board of Governors of the Federal Reserve System. Financial stability report. Federal Reserve Board report, available at https://www.federalreserve.gov/publications/files/financial-stability-report-20211108.pdf, November 2021.

[27]  Doug Brain, Michiel De Pooter, Dobrislav Dobrev, Michael Fleming, Pete Johansson, Collin Jones, Frank Keane, Michael Puglia, Liza Reiderman, Tony Rodrigues, and Or Shachar. Unlocking the Treasury market through TRACE. FEDS Notes, available at https://www.federalreserve.gov/econres/notes/feds-notes/unlocking-the-treasury-market-through-trace-20180928.htm, September 2018.

[28]  Lael Brainard. Some preliminary financial stability lessons from the COVID-19 shock. Speech at the 2021 Annual Washington Conference Institute of International Bankers, Board of Governors of the Federal Reserve System, available at https://www.federalreserve.gov/newsevents/speech/files/brainard20210301a.pdf, March 2021.

[29]  Johannes Breckenfelder and Victoria Ivashina. Bank leverage constraints and bond market illiquidity during the COVID-19 crisis. European Central Bank Research Bulletin Number 89, available at https://www.ecb.europa.eu/pub/economic-research/resbull/2021/html/ecb.rb211124d9e3f578d2.en.html, November 2021.

[30]  Markus K. Brunnermeier and Lasse Heje Pedersen. Market liquidity and funding liquidity. *The Review of Financial Studies*, 22(6):2201–2238, 2009.

[31]  Analisa Bucalossi and Antonio Scalia. Leverage ratio, central bank operations and repo market. Questioni di Economia e Finanza, Occasional Paper Number 347, available at https://papers.ssrn.com/sol3/papers.cfm?abstract_id=2863903, July 2016.

[32]  Katy Burne. How to succeed in fixing settlement fails. BNY Mellon Aerial View Report, available at https://www.bnymellon.com/content/dam/bnymellon/documents/pdf/aerial-view/how-to-succeed-in-fixing-settlement-fails.pdf, October 2020.

[33]  Matt Cameron. JP Morgan takes $1.5 billion funding valuation adjustment loss. *Risk*, available at http://www.risk.net/risk-magazine/news/2322843/jp-morgan-takes-usd15-billion-fva-loss, January 2014.

[34] Center for Economic Policy Studies Task Force. European bank resolution: Making it work. Interim Report of the CEPS Task Force on Implementing Financial Sector Resolution, available at https://papers.ssrn.com/sol3/papers.cfm?abstract_id=2723220, January 2016.

[35] Daniel Chen and Darrell Duffie. Market fragmentation. *American Economic Review*, 111(7):2247–2274, 2021.

[36] Jessie Ziqing Chen, Johannes Chen, Shamarthi Ghosh, Manu Pandey, and Adrian Walton. Potential netting benefits from expanded central clearing in Canada's fixed-income market. Staff Analytical Note, available at https://www.bankofcanada.ca/2022/06/staff-analytical-note-2022-8/, June 2022.

[37] Jeffrey Cheng, David Wessel, and Joshua Younger. How did COVID-19 disrupt the market for US Treasury debt? Hutchins Center, Brookings Institution, available at https://www.brookings.edu/blog/up-front/2020/05/01/how-did-covid-19-disrupt-the-market-for-u-s-treasury-debt/, May 2020.

[38] Jaewon Choi and Yesol Huh. Customer liquidity provision: Implications for corporate bond transaction costs. Working paper, Federal Reserve Board, available at https://papers.ssrn.com/sol3/papers.cfm?abstract_id=3081747, September 2017.

[39] Richard Clarida, Burcu Duygan-Bump, and Chiara Scotti. The COVID-19 crisis and the Federal Reserve's policy response. Finance and Economics Discussion Series 2021-035, available at https://www.federalreserve.gov/econres/feds/files/2021035pap.pdf, June 2021.

[40] Kevin Clark, Antoine Martin, and Tim Wessel. The Federal Reserve's large-scale repo program. *Liberty Street Economics*, Federal Reserve Bank of New York, available at https://libertystreeteconomics.newyorkfed.org/2020/08/the-federal-reserves-large-scale-repo-program.html, August 2020.

[41] Jean-Edouard Colliard and Thierry Foucault. Trading fees and efficiency in limit order markets. *Review of Financial Studies*, 25:3389–3421, 2012.

[42] Pierre Collin-Dufresne, Benjamin Junge, and Anders B. Trolle. Market structure and transaction costs of index CDSs. *Journal of Finance*, 75(5):2719–2763, 2020.

[43] Carole Comerton-Forde, Terry Hendershott, Charles Jones, Pamela Moulton, and Mark Seasholes. Time variation in liquidity: The role of market-maker inventories and revenues. *Journal of Finance*, 65:295–331, 2010.

[44] Committee on Capital Markets Regulation. Nothing but the facts: The US Treasury Market during the COVID-19 crisis. Committee on Capital Markets Regulation Report, available at https://www.capmktsreg.org/wp-content/uploads/2021/03/NBTF-US-Treasury-Markets-During-Covid.pdf, March 2021.

[45] Richard Comotto. Repo and CCP client clearing. Finadium Report, available at https://finadium.com/finadium-repo-and-ccp-client-clearing/, February 2021.

[46] Congressional Budget Office. The 2022 long-term budget outlook. Congressional Budget Office report, available at https://www.cbo.gov/system/files/2022-07/57971-LTBO.pdf, July 2022.

[47] Harry Cooperman, Darrell Duffie, Stephan Luck, Zachry Wang, and Yilin Yang. Bank funding risk, reference rates, and credit supply. Working paper, Graduate School of Business, Stanford University, August 2022.

[48] Adam Copeland, Darrell Duffie, and Yilin Yang. Reserves were not so ample after all. Working paper, Graduate School of Business, Stanford University, available at https://papers.ssrn.com/sol3/papers.cfm?abstract_id=3897525, July 2022.

[49] Hans Degryse, Frank De Jong, and Vincent van Kervel. The impact of dark trading and visible fragmentation on market quality. *Review of Finance*, 19(4):1587–1622, 2015.

[50] Jens Dick-Nielsen and Marco Rossi. The cost of immediacy for corporate bonds. *The Review of Financial Studies*, 32(1):1–41, 2019.

[51]   Jamie Dimon. Letter to shareholders of JPMorgan. JP Morgan, available at https://www.jpmorganchase.com/content/dam/jpmc/jpmorgan-chase-and-co/investor-relations/documents/ceo-letter-to-shareholders-2020.pdf, April 2021.

[52]   DTCC. More clearing, less risk: Increasing centrally cleared activity in the US Treasury cash market. White paper, DTCC, available at https://www.dtcc.com/-/media/Files/PDFs/DTCC-US-Treasury-Whitepaper.pdf, May 2021.

[53]   Wenxin Du, Alexander Tepper, and Adrien Verdelan. Deviations from covered interest rate parity. *Journal of Finance*, 73(3):915–957, 2018.

[54]   Wenxin Du, Benjamin Hebert, and Wenhao Li. Intermediary balance sheets and the Treasury yield curve. Working paper, National Bureau of Economic Research, available at https://papers.ssrn.com/sol3/papers.cfm?abstract_id=4159135, July 2022.

[55]   Darrell Duffie. Market making under the proposed Volcker Rule. Rock Center for Corporate Governance at Stanford University Working Paper, Report to the Securities Industry and Financial Markets Association, and Submission to the Office of the Comptroller of the Currency, the Board of Governors of the Federal Reserve System, the Federal Deposit Insurance Corporation, and the Securities and Exchange Commission, available at https://papers.ssrn.com/sol3/papers.cfm?abstract_id=1990472, January 2012.

[56]   Darrell Duffie. Has something gone wrong with over-the-counter markets? *Banking Perspectives*, 5(2):56–61, 2017.

[57]   Darrell Duffie. Financial regulatory reform after the crisis: An assessment. *Management Science*, 64(10):4471–4965, 2018.

[58]   Darrell Duffie. Prone to fail: The pre-crisis financial system. *Journal of Economic Perspectives*, 33:81–106, 2019.

[59]   Darrell Duffie. Still the world's safe haven? – Redesigning the US Treasury market after the COVID-19 crisis. Hutchins Center Working Paper Number 62, Brookings Institution, available at https://www.brookings.edu/wp-content/uploads/2020/05/WP62_Duffie_updated.pdf, May 2020.

[60]   Darrell Duffie and Arvind Krishnamurthy. Passthrough efficiency in the Fed's new monetary policy setting. In Richard Babson, editor, *Designing Resilient Monetary Policy Frameworks for the Future, A Symposium Sponsored by the Federal Reserve Bank of Kansas City*, pages 21–102. Federal Reserve Bank of Kansas City, 2016.

[61]   Darrell Duffie and Haoxiang Zhu. Size discovery. *Review of Financial Studies*, 30:1095–1150, 2017.

[62]   Darrell Duffie, Pitor Dworczak, and Haoxiang Zhu. Benchmarks in search markets. *Journal of Finance*, 72:2017–2044, 2017.

[63]   Louis Ederington, Wei Guan, and Pradeep Yadav. Dealer spreads in the corporate bond market: Agent versus market-making roles. Working paper, University of Oklahoma, available at https://papers.ssrn.com/sol3/papers.cfm?abstract_id=2378000, July 2021.

[64]   Amy Edwards, Larry Harris, and Michael Piwowar. Corporate bond market transaction costs and transparency. *Journal of Finance*, 62:1421–1451, 2007.

[65]   James Egelhof, Antoine Martin, and Noah Zinsmeister. Regulatory incentives and quarter-end dynamics in the repo market. *Liberty Street Economics*, available at https://libertystreeteconomics.newyorkfed.org/2017/08/regulatory-incentives-and-quarter-end-dynamics-in-the-repo-market/, August 2017.

[66]   Thomas Eisenbach and Gregory Phelan. Fragility of safe asset markets. Federal Reserve Bank of New York Staff Report Number 1023, available at https://papers.ssrn.com/sol3/papers.cfm?abstract_id=4164189, July 2022.

[67]   Egemen Eren and Philip Wooldridge. Non-bank financial institutions and the functioning of government bond markets. Bank for International Settlements, BIS Paper Number 119, available at https://www.bis.org/publ/bppdf/bispap119.htm, November 2021.

[68] Ernst and Young. Reflecting credit and funding adjustments in fair value: A survey, available at http://www.ey.com/GL/en/Newsroom/News-releases/News_Impact-of-regulatory-and-accounting-changes-critical-to-viability-of-banks-OTC-derivatives-business, Spring 2012.

[69] Antonio Falato, Itay Goldstein, and Ali Hortacsu. Financial fragility in the COVID-19 crisis: The case of investment funds in corporate bond markets. *Journal of Monetary Economics*, 123:35–52, 2021.

[70] Giovanni Favara, Sebastian Infante, and Marcelo Rezende. Leverage regulations and Treasury market participation: Evidence from credit line drawdowns. Working paper, Federal Reserve Board of Governors, available at https://drive.google.com/file/d/12_l_0e8P8D4N2fHs-LS6hBgCZFarY57s/view, June 2022.

[71] Federal Register. Prohibitions and restrictions on proprietary trading and certain interests in, and relationships with, hedge funds and private equity funds. Federal Register, available at https://www.federalregister.gov/documents/2020/07/31/2020-15525/prohibitions-and-restrictions-on-proprietary-trading-and-certain-interests-in-and-relationships-with, January 2014.

[72] Federal Reserve Bank of New York. The June 2022 senior credit officer opinion survey on dealer financing terms. Federal Reserve Bank of New York Senior Credit Officer Opinion Survey, available at https://www.federalreserve.gov/data/scoos/scoos-202206.htm, June 2022.

[73] Financial Stability Board. Holistic review of the March market turmoil. Financial Stability Board reports to the G20, available at https://www.fsb.org/2020/11/holistic-review-of-the-march-market-turmoil/, November 2020.

[74] Michael Fleming. Treasury market liquidity and the Federal Reserve during the COVID-19 pandemic. *Liberty Street Economics*, Federal Reserve Bank of New York, available at https://libertystreeteconomics.newyorkfed.org/2020/05/treasury-market-liquidity-and-the-federal-reserve-during-the-covid-19-pandemic.html, May 2020.

[75] Michael Fleming and Frank Keane. The netting efficiencies of marketwide central clearing. Federal Reserve Bank of New York, Staff Report Number 964, available at https://www.newyorkfed.org/research/staff_reports/sr964, April 2021.

[76] Michael Fleming and Giang Nguyen. Price and size discovery in financial markets: Evidence from the US Treasury securities market. *The Review of Asset Pricing Studies*, 9(2):256–295, 2019.

[77] Michael Fleming and Francisco Ruela. Treasury market liquidity during the COVID-19 Crisis. *Liberty Street Economics*, Federal Reserve Bank of New York, available at https://libertystreeteconomics.newyorkfed.org/2020/04/treasury-market-liquidity-during-the-covid-19-crisis.html, April 2020.

[78] Michael Fleming, Frank Keane, Antoine Martin, and Michael McMorrow. Measuring settlement fails. *Liberty Street Economics*, Federal Reserve Bank of New York, available at https://libertystreeteconomics.newyorkfed.org/2014/09/measuring-settlement-fails.html, September 2014.

[79] Michael Fleming, Haoyang Liu, Rich Podjasek, and Jack Schurmeier. The Federal Reserve's market functioning purchases. Federal Bank of New York Staff Report Number 998, available at https://papers.ssrn.com/sol3/papers.cfm?abstract_id=3992583, December 2021.

[80] Jean-Sebastien Fontaine, Corey Garriott, Jesse Johal, Jessica Lee, and Andreas Uthemann. COVID-19 crisis: Lessons learned for future policy research. Staff Discussion Paper, Bank of Canada, available at https://www.bankofcanada.ca/2021/02/staff-discussion-paper-2021-2/, February 2021.

[81] Kenneth Garbade. The evolution of repo contracting conventions in the 1980s. *FRBNY Economic Policy Review*, 12(1):27–42, 2006.

[82]   Kenneth Garbade. *After the Accord: A History of Federal Reserve Open Market Operations, the US Government Securities market, and Treasury Debt Management from 1951 to 1979.* Cambridge University Press, January 2021.

[83]   Kenneth Garbade and Frank Keane. Market function purchases by the Federal Reserve. *Liberty Street Economics*, Federal Reserve Bank of New York, available at https://libertystreeteconomics.newyorkfed.org/2020/08/market-function-purchases-by-the-federal-reserve.html, August 2020.

[84]   Eddie Gerba and Petros Katsoulis. The repo market under Basel III. Bank of England working paper, available at https://papers.ssrn.com/sol3/papers.cfm?abstract_id=4012925, May 2022.

[85]   Christina Getz, Julie Remache, Kathryn Chen, Lisa Stowe, Radhika Mithal, Karen Brifu, and Timothy Chu. Open market operations during 2020. Report prepared for the Federal Open Market Committee by the Markets Group of the Federal Reserve Bank of New York, available at https://www.newyorkfed.org/medialibrary/media/markets/omo/omo2020-pdf.pdf, May 2021.

[86]   Jonathan Goldberg. Dealer inventory constraints during the COVID-19 pandemic: Evidence from the Treasury market and broader implications. FEDS Notes. Washington: Board of Governors of the Federal Reserve System, available at https://www.federalreserve.gov/econres/notes/feds-notes/dealer-inventory-constraints-during-covid-19-pandemic-evidence-from-treasury-market-broader-implications-20200717.htm, July 2020.

[87]   Jonathan Goldberg. Liquidity supply by broker-dealers and real activity. *Journal of Finance*, 136:806–827, 2020.

[88]   Jonathan Goldberg and Yoshio Nozawa. Liquidity supply in the corporate bond market. *Journal of Finance*, 76(2):755–796, 2021.

[89]   Michael Goldstein, Edith Hotchkiss, and Erik Sirri. Transparency and liquidity: A controlled experiment on corporate bonds. *Review of Financial Studies*, 20:235–273, 2007.

[90]   Government Accounting Office. Federal debt management: Treasury quickly financed historic government response to the pandemic and is assessing risks to market functioning. GAO Report to Congressional Committees, available at https://www.gao.gov/assets/gao-21-606.pdf, August 2021.

[91]   Sandy Grossman and Merton Miller. Liquidity and market structure. *Journal of Finance*, 43:617–633, 1988.

[92]   Group of Thirty. US Treasury markets: Steps toward increased resilience. G30 Working Group on Treasury Market Liquidity, Group of 30, Washington, DC, available at https://group30.org/images/uploads/publications/G30_U.S_._Treasury_Markets-_Steps_Toward_Increased_Resilience__1.pdf, July 2021.

[93]   Group of Thirty. US Treasury markets: Steps toward increased resilience status update 2022. G30 Special Report, available at https://group30.org/images/uploads/publications/G30_Treasury-Mkts-UPDATE_Final_Report.pdf, June 2022.

[94]   Valentin Haddad, Alan Moreira, and Tyler Muir. When selling becomes viral: Disruptions in debt markets in the COVID-19 Crisis and the Fed's response. *The Review of Financial Studies*, 34(11):5309–5351, 2021.

[95]   James Collin Harkrader and Michael Puglia. Price discovery in the US Treasury cash market: On principal trading firms and dealers. Board of Governors of the Federal Reserve Board, FEDS working paper, available at https://www.federalreserve.gov/econres/feds/files/2020096pap.pdf, October 2020.

[96]   Larry Harris. Transactions costs, trade throughs, and riskless principal trading in corporate bond markets. Working Paper, University of Southern California, available at https://papers.ssrn.com/sol3/papers.cfm?abstract_id=2661801, October 2015.

[97]   Andrew Hauser. Seven moments in Spring: COVID-19, financial markets and the
       Bank of England's balance sheet operations. Speech, Bank of England, available
       at https://www.bankofengland.co.uk/-/media/boe/files/speech/2020/seven-
       moments-in-spring-covid-19-speech-by-andrew-hauser.pdf?la=en&hash=
       43D022917D76095F1E79CBDD5D42FCD96497EA5F, June 2020.
[98]   Andrew Hauser. From lender of last resort to market maker of last resort via the dash for
       cash: Why central banks need new tools for dealing with market dysfunction. Speech given
       at Thomson Reuters Newsmaker, Bank of England, available at https://www.bankofengland.
       co.uk/speech/2021/january/andrew-hauser-speech-at-thomson-reuters-newsmaker, January
       2021.
[99]   Zhiguo He, Bryan Kelly, and Asaf Manela. Intermediary asset pricing: New evidence from
       many asset classes. *Journal of Financial Economics*, 126(1):1–35, 2017.
[100]  Zhiguo He, Stefan Nagel, and Zhaogang Song. Treasury inconvenience yields during the
       COVID-19 crisis. *Journal of Financial Economics*, 143(1):57–79, 2020.
[101]  Jean Helwege and Liying Wang. Liquidity and price pressure in the corporate bond market:
       Evidence from mega-bonds. *Journal of Financial Intermediation*, 48, 100922, 2021.
[102]  Terry Hendershott and Ananth Madhavan. Click or call? Auction versus search in the
       over-the-counter market. *Journal of Finance*, 70:419–447, 2015.
[103]  Grace Xing Hu, Jun Pan, and Jiang Wang. Noise as information for illiquidity. *Journal of
       Finance*, 68:2341–2382, 2013.
[104]  Wenqian Huang and Elöd Takáts. The CCP-bank nexus at the time of COVID-19. *BIS Bulletin*,
       Number 13, pp. 1–7, May 2020.
[105]  Glenn Hubbard, Donald Kohn, Laurie Goodman, Kathryn Judge, Anil Kashyap, Ralph Koijen,
       Blythe Masters, Sandie O'Connor, and Kara Stein. Task force on financial stability. Report
       by the Hutchins Center on Fiscal and Monetary Policy at Brookings, available at https:
       //www.brookings.edu/wp-content/uploads/2021/06/financial-stability_report.pdf, June
       2021.
[106]  ICMA European Repo Council. Perspectives from the eye of the storm: The current state and
       future evolution of the European repo market. Initiative of the ICMA European Repo Council,
       available at https://www.icmagroup.org/assets/documents/Regulatory/Repo/The-current-
       state-and-future-evolution-of-the-European-repo-market-181115.pdf, November 2015.
[107]  Jane Ihrig. Banks' demand for reserves in the face of liquidity regulations. *On the Economy
       Blog*, Federal Reserve Bank of St. Louis, available at https://www.stlouisfed.org/on-the-
       economy/2019/march/banks-demand-reserves-face-liquidity-regulations, March 2019.
[108]  Jane Ihrig, Zeynep Senyuz, and Gretchen Weinbach. The Fed's "Ample-Reserves" approach to
       implementing monetary policy. FEDS Working Paper, available https://www.federalreserve.
       gov/econres/feds/files/2020022pap.pdf, February 2020.
[109]  Jeffrey Ingber. The development of the Government Securities Clearing Corporation. *FRBNY
       Economic Policy Review*, 23(2):33–50, 2017, available at https://www.newyorkfed.org/
       medialibrary/media/research/epr/2017/epr_2017_gscc_ingber.pdf?la=en, December 2017.
[110]  Inter-Agency Working Group for Treasury Market Surveillance. Recent disruptions and
       potential reforms in the US Treasury market: A staff progress report. Joint Report, available
       at https://home.treasury.gov/system/files/136/IAWG-Treasury-Report.pdf, November 2021.
[111]  International Capital Market Association. European repo market survey. ICMA, Zurich,
       available at https://www.icmagroup.org/assets/documents/Market-Info/Repo-Market-
       Surveys/No.-32-December-2016/RepoSurvey-140217.pdf, February 2017.
[112]  ISDA. Swapsinfo quarterly review, available at https://www.isda.org/a/6BagE/SwapsInfo-
       First-Half-of-2022-and-the-Second-Quarter-of-2022-Review-Full-Report.pdf. International
       Swaps and Derivatives Association, August 2022.

[113] Michael Jensen and William Meckling. Theory of the firm: Managerial behavior, agency costs and ownership structure. *Journal of Financial Economics*, 3:305–360, 1976.

[114] Jay Kahn and Vy Nguyen. Treasury market stress: Lessons from 1958 and today. Office of Financial Research Brief Series, available at https://www.financialresearch.gov/briefs/files/OFRBr_22-01_Treasury_Market_Stress_Lessons_from_1958_and_Today_061622.pdf, June 2022.

[115] Jay Kahn and Luke Olson. Who participates in cleared repo? Office of Financial Research Brief, available at https://www.financialresearch.gov/briefs/files/OFRBr_21-01_Repo.pdf, July 2021.

[116] Mahyar Kargar, Benjamin Lester, David Lindsay, Shuo Liu, Pierre-Olivier Weill, and Diego Zúñiga. Corporate bond liquidity during the COVID-19 Crisis. *The Review of Financial Studies*, 34(11):5352–5401, 2021.

[117] John Maynard Keynes. *A Tract on Monetary Reform*. Macmillan, London, 1923.

[118] Ilkka Kiema and Esa Jokivuolle. Does a leverage ratio requirement increase bank stability? *Journal of Banking and Finance*, 39:240–254, 2014.

[119] Sven Klingler and Suresh Sundaresan. Diminishing Treasury convenience premiums: Effects of dealers' excess demand in auctions. Working paper, BI Norwegian Business School and Columbia University, available at https://papers.ssrn.com/sol3/papers.cfm?abstract_id=3556502, March 2022.

[120] KPMG. FVA: Putting funding into the equation, available at https://assets.kpmg/content/dam/kpmg/pdf/2014/01/putting-funding-equation-dec-13.pdf, December 2013.

[121] Mathias S. Kruttli, Philip Monin, Lubomir Petrasek, and Sumudu W. Watugala. Hedge fund Treasury trading and funding fragility: Evidence from the COVID-19 crisis. Working paper, available at https://papers.ssrn.com/sol3/papers.cfm?abstract_id=3817978, April 2021.

[122] Nellie Liang and Pat Parkinson. Enhancing liquidity of the US Treasury market under stress. Hutchins Center Working Paper 72, available at https://www.brookings.edu/research/enhancing-liquidity-of-the-u-s-treasury-market-under-stress/, December 2020.

[123] Antoine Martin. Reform, regulation, and changes in the US repo market. Presentation, Federal Reserve Bank of New York, April 2016.

[124] Andrew Metrick and Daniel K. Tarullo. Congruent financial regulation. Brookings Papers on Economic Activity Conference Drafts, available at https://www.brookings.edu/wp-content/uploads/2021/03/BPEASP21_Metrick-Tarullo_conf-draft.pdf, March 2021.

[125] Merton Miller. Do the M&M propositions apply to banks? *Journal of Banking and Finance*, 19:483–489, 1995.

[126] Bruce Mizrach. Analysis of corporate bond liquidity. Research Note, FINRA Office of the Chief Economist, available at https://www.finra.org/sites/default/files/OCE_researchnote_liquidity_2015_12.pdf, December 2015.

[127] Franco Modigliani and Merton Miller. The cost of capital, corporation finance and the theory of investment. *The American Economic Review*, 48:261–297, 1958.

[128] Stephen Morris. Barclays agrees to offload derivatives contracts to JP Morgan. Bloomberg, available at http://www.bloomberg.com/news/articles/2016-02-03/barclays-agrees-to-offload-derivatives-contracts-to-jpmorgan, February 2016.

[129] Benjamin Munyan. Regulatory arbitrage in repo markets. OFR Working Paper 15–22, Office of Financial Research, available at https://papers.ssrn.com/sol3/papers.cfm?abstract_id=2685592, September 2017.

[130] Stewart Myers. Determinants of corporate borrowing. *Journal of Financial Economics*, 5:147–175, 1977.

[131] Mahendrarajah Nimalendran and Sugata Ray. Informational linkages between dark and lit trading venues. *Journal of Financial Markets*, 17:230–261, 2014.

[132] Roman Pancs. Workup. *Review of Economic Design*, 18(1):37–71, 2014.

[133] Joe Parsons. Barclays offloads non-core derivatives to JP Morgan. The Trade, available at http: //www.thetradenews.com/Sell-side/Barclays-offloads-non-core-derivatives-to-JP-Morgan/, February 2016.

[134] Jerome Powell. Central clearing and liquidity. Speech at the Federal Reserve Bank of Chicago Symposium on Central Clearing, Federal Reserve Board of Governors, available at https: //www.federalreserve.gov/newsevents/speech/powell20170623a.htm, June 2017.

[135] Murray Pozmanter. US Treasuries clearing challenge finding the right incentives. DTCC, available at https://www.dtcc.com/dtcc-connection/articles/2020/december/03/us-treasuries-clearing-challenge-finding-the-right-incentives, December 2020.

[136] Zoltan Pozsar. Collateral supply and o/n rates. Global Money Notes 22, Credit Suisse Economics, May, 2019.

[137] Principal Traders Group. Clearing a path to a more resilient Treasury market. FIA Principal Traders Group, available at https://www.fia.org/sites/default/files/2021-07/FIA-PTG_Paper_ResilientJuly2021.

[138] Dagfinn Rime, Andreas Schrimpf, and Olav Syrstad. Segmented money markets and covered interest parity arbitrage. BIS working paper Number 651, available at https://www.bis.org/publ/work651.htm, September 2017.

[139] Brian Ruane. The future of wholesale funding markets. BNY Mellon, available at https://www.asifma.org/wp-content/uploads/2018/05/the-future-of-wholesale-funding-markets.pdf, December 2015.

[140] Brian Ruane. The pandemic stress test: US government securities clearance and repo. BNY Mellon Report, available at https://info.bnymellon.com/rs/651-GHF-471/images/PANDEMICSTRESSTEST_FINAL.pdf, August 2020.

[141] Andreas Schrimpf, Hyun Song Shin, and Vladyslav Sushko. Leverage and margin spirals in fixed income markets during the COVID-19 crisis. *BIS Bulletin*, Number 2, pp. 1–6, April 2020.

[142] Hal Scott, John Gulliver, Jon Ondrejko, and Samuel Holt. Mandatory central clearing for US Treasuries and US Treasury repos. Program on International Financial Systems report, available at https://www.pifsinternational.org/wp-content/uploads/2021/11/PIFS-Mandatory-Central-Clearing-for-US-Treasury-Markets-11.11.2021.pdf, November 2021.

[143] Securities and Exchange Commission. SEC proposes amendments to include significant Treasury markets platforms within regulation ATS. SEC press release, available at https: //www.sec.gov/news/press-release/2022-10, January 2022.

[144] Nazneen Sherif. Banks launch drive to crush outsized XVAs. *Risk*, available at http://www.risk.net/risk-magazine/comment/2448322/banks-launch-drive-to-crush-outsized-xvas, February 2016.

[145] Nazneen Sherif. Banks turn to synthetic derivatives to cut initial margin. *Risk*, available at http://www.risk.net/derivatives/5290756/banks-turn-to-synthetic-derivatives-to-cut-initial-margin, June 2017.

[146] SIFMA. SIFMA electronic bond trading report: US corporate and municipal securities. Securities Industry and Financial Market Association, available at https://www.sifma.org/resources/general/electronic-bond-trading-report-us-corporate-and-municipal-securities/, February 2016.

[147] Yang Song. Dealer funding costs: Implications for the term structure of dividend risk premia. Working paper, Stanford University, available at http://ssrn.com/abstract=2732133, January 2016.

[148] The Brattle Group. Summary of responses to the 2022 ISDA UST survey regarding ongoing efforts to incentivize and/or potentially require additional clearing of US Treasury (UST) securities and repos. A report prepared by the Brattle Group for ISDA, August 2022.

[149] Treasury Borrowing Advisory Committee. Revisiting Treasury buybacks. TBAC Charge, US Treasury Department, available at https://home.treasury.gov/system/files/221/TBACCharge2Q32022.pdf, August 2022.

[150] Treasury Market Practices Group. Clearing and settlement in the secured financing transaction market. TMPG draft work product, available at https://www.newyorkfed.org/medialibrary/ Microsites/tmpg/files/CSP_SFT_Draft_Maps.pdf, November 2021.

[151] Treasury Market Practices Group. TMPG releases updates for working groups on clearing and settlement practices for Treasury SFTs, Treasury market data and transparency. TMPG draft work product, available at https://www.newyorkfed.org/medialibrary/Microsites/tmpg/ files/DT_Draft_Catalogues.pdf, November 2021.

[152] Treasury Markets Practices Group. White paper on clearing and settlement in the secondary market for US Treasury securities. TMPG Consultative Paper, Federal Reserve Bank of New York, available at https://www.newyorkfed.org/medialibrary/Microsites/tmpg/files/CS-DraftPaper-071218.pdf, July 2018.

[153] Treasury Markets Practices Group. Best practice guidance on clearing and settlement. TMPG Consultative Paper, Federal Reserve Bank of New York, available at https://www.newyorkfed. org/medialibrary/Microsites/tmpg/files/CS_BestPractices_071119.pdf, July 2019.

[154] Francesco Trebbi and Kairong Xiao. Regulation and market liquidity. *Management Science*, 65(5):2019–2443, 2019.

[155] US Department of the Treasury. A financial system that creates economic opportunities capital markets – Report to President Donald J. Trump on core principles for regulating the United States financial system. Treasury Department, Washington DC, available at https://www.treasury.gov/press-center/press-releases/Documents/A-Financial-System-Capital-Markets-FINAL-FINAL.pdf, October 2017.

[156] US Department of the Treasury and Federal Reserve. Report of the joint Treasury-Federal Reserve study of the US government securities market. Joint Report by the US Treasury and the Federal Reserve, available at https://fraser.stlouisfed.org/title/joint-treasury-federal-reserve-study-us-government-securities-market-318/report-joint-treasury-federal-reserve-study-us-government-securities-market-6282, April 1969.

[157] US Department of the Treasury, Board of Governors of the Federal Reserve System, Federal Reserve Bank of New York, US Securities and Exchange Commission, and US Commodity Futures Trading Commission. Joint staff report on the US Treasury market. Washington DC, available at https://www.treasury.gov/press-center/press-releases/Documents/Joint_Staff_Report_Treasury_10-15-2015.pdf, July 2015.

[158] Annette Vissing-Jorgensen. The Treasury market in Spring 2020 and the response of the Federal Reserve. *Journal of Monetary Economics*, 124:19–47, 2021.

[159] Sebastian Vogel. When to introduce electronic trading platforms in over-the-counter Markets? Working paper, Ecole Polytechnique Fédérale de Lausanne, available at https://papers.ssrn. com/sol3/papers.cfm?abstract_id=2895222, December 2017.

[160] Chaojun Wang. Core-periphery trading networks. Working paper, Stanford University, available at https://web.stanford.edu/chaojunw/papers/Wang_CorePeriphery.pdf, February 2017.

[161] Xingjie Wang, Yangru Wu, Hongjun Yan, and Zhandong Zhong. Funding liquidity shocks in a natural experiment: Evidence from the CDS Big Bang. Working paper, Southern University of Science and Technology, available at http://papers.ssrn.com/sol3/papers.cfm?abstract_id=2730877, September 2016.

[162] Duncan Wood. How FVA saved the cross-currency swap. *Risk*, available at http://www.risk. net/risk-magazine/opinion/2440243/how-fva-saved-the-cross-currency-swap, January 2016.

[163] Haoxiang Zhu. Finding a good price in opaque over-the-counter markets. *Review of Financial Studies*, 25(4):1255–1285, 2012.

[164] Haoxiang Zhu. Do dark pools harm price discovery? *Review of Financial Studies*, 27:747–789, 2013.

www.ingramcontent.com/pod-product-compliance
Lightning Source LLC
Chambersburg PA
CBHW062014210326
41458CB00075B/5417